NEW DIRECTIONS FOR COMMUNITY COLLEGES

Arthur M. Cohen
EDITOR-IN-CHIEF

Florence B. Brawer
ASSOCIATE EDITOR

The Viability of the Private Junior College

Robert H. Woodroof
Pepperdine University

EDITOR

Number 69, Spring 1990

JOSSEY-BASS INC., PUBLISHERS
San Francisco • Oxford

The Viability of the Private Junior College.
Robert H. Woodroof (ed.).
New Directions for Community Colleges, no. 69.
Volume XVIII, number 1.

NEW DIRECTIONS FOR COMMUNITY COLLEGES
Arthur M. Cohen, Editor-in-Chief; *Florence B. Brawer,* Associate Editor

Copyright © 1990 by Jossey-Bass Inc., Publishers
and
Jossey-Bass Limited

Copyright under International, Pan American, and Universal Copyright Conventions. All rights reserved. No part of this issue may be reproduced in any form—except for a brief quotation (not to exceed 500 words) in a review or professional work—without permission in writing from the publishers.

NEW DIRECTIONS FOR COMMUNITY COLLEGES is part of The Jossey-Bass Higher Education Series and is published quarterly by Jossey-Bass Inc., Publishers (publication number USPS 121-710) in association with the ERIC Clearinghouse for Junior Colleges. Second-class postage paid at San Francisco, California, and at additional mailing offices. Postmaster: Send address changes to Jossey-Bass Inc., Publishers, 350 Sansome Street, San Francisco, California 94104.

THE MATERIAL in this publication is based on work sponsored wholly or in part by the Office of Educational Research and Improvement, U.S. Department of Education, under contract number RI-88-062002. Its contents do not necessarily reflect the views of the Department, or any other agency of the U.S. Government.

EDITORIAL CORRESPONDENCE should be sent to the Editor-in-Chief, Arthur M. Cohen, ERIC Clearinghouse for Junior Colleges, University of California, Los Angeles, California 90024.

Library of Congress Catalog Card Number LC 85-644753

International Standard Serial Number ISSN 0194-3081

International Standard Book Number ISBN 1-55542-822-3

Cover photograph by Rene Sheret, Los Angeles, California © 1990.

Manufactured in the United States of America. Printed on acid-free paper.

Contents

Editor's Notes 1
Robert H. Woodroof

1. A History of Resilience 3
Robert H. Woodroof
Once a valued partner in America's push for egalitarianism in higher education, the private junior college is fighting to survive the century.

2. The Private Junior College in Higher Education's Future 9
Nelson M. Hoffman, Jr.
Leaders of America's private junior colleges are cautiously optimistic about the future but admit that the concerns are serious and life-threatening.

3. A Professional Approach to Marketing the Private Junior College 19
Peter T. Mitchell
Sophisticated marketing techniques, differentiation, and innovation are keys to growth in the 1990s.

4. Assessment, the Affordable Way 33
John H. Williams
A workable approach to assessing the value-added benefits of a private junior college education can be developed, even with limited resources.

5. Expanding the Religious Heterogeneity of the Student Body 43
George D. Fields, Jr.
The church-related junior college must become less sectarian and more heterogeneous in recruitment and academic development.

6. Instructional Use of Computers in the Junior College 57
Gordon L. Wells
To be competitive in the race for students and honest in its boast of providing a quality education, the private junior college must find the resources to bring itself into the computer age.

7. The Adjunct/Full-Time Faculty Ratio 71
Milton L. Smith
Trends indicate that the current practice of hiring a large percentage of adjunct faculty in private junior colleges will continue for the foreseeable future. Efforts must be made to enhance the benefits and reduce the detriments of the practice.

8. **Doubts About the Future of the Private Liberal Arts Junior College** 83
Robert H. Woodroof
If trends continue, two-thirds of today's private junior colleges will not survive the 1990s.

INDEX 93

Editor's Notes

The debate concerning the future of the private liberal arts junior college follows three tracks:

1. Can the private junior college survive into the twenty-first century as a distinct alternative to the first two years of the college experience?
2. What must the private junior college do to survive into the twenty-first century?
3. Can the private junior college coexist successfully with the community college in an educational system saturated with colleges, universities, proprietary schools, and many other forms of educational opportunity?

This volume attempts to address each of these issues. In Chapter One, I set the stage for the debate by giving a brief review of the colorful history of the private junior college, particularly its role in the development of egalitarianism in higher education within the United States.

In Chapters Two and Eight, the future survival of the private junior college is debated. In Chapter Two, Nelson M. Hoffman, Jr., presents a cautiously optimistic view of the future in the midst of formidable obstacles and concerns. My concerns regarding the future of this unique sector of higher education, as described in Chapter Eight, could be considered "cautiously pessimistic." These two chapters are not diametric to each other, particularly with regard to the value of the private junior college, but they do give distinctly different views of the future.

Chapters Three, Four, and Five address the issue of how to ensure survival. In Chapter Three, Peter T. Mitchell draws from his experience in developing a marketing model specifically for the private junior college. John H. Williams, in Chapter Four, discusses the increasingly popular issue of student assessment, focusing on the most efficient ways to document student achievement resulting from the private junior college experience. One of the prominent strengths of the private junior college is its ability to prepare students for leadership roles and advanced academic study. Documenting this strength with accurate data may help many private junior colleges overcome the discouraging trend toward closure that has characterized this segment of higher education for nearly five decades.

In Chapter Five, George D. Fields, Jr., encourages church-related junior colleges to step out of denominational sectarianism in their educational missions and provide an educational environment for students from many religious backgrounds. This is particularly important during a time when prospective student pools are shrinking and creative recruiting strategies are essential for survival.

Chapters Six and Seven discuss cooperation between private junior colleges and community colleges, although not specifically in light of the survival of the private junior college. In Chapter Six, Gordon L. Wells examines the important issue of computer technology and its integration into the entire junior college curriculum. His view is that private junior colleges cannot afford to ignore this resource if they want to compete in providing undergraduate education.

Milton L. Smith discusses in Chapter Seven the adjunct/full-time faculty ratio, an important concern for many private junior colleges and community colleges. The optimum ratio is elusive, but the accurate distribution of faculty is vital for balancing cost and quality in the private junior college educational process.

Together, the eight chapters in this volume address the status of the private junior college and the issues that must be faced if survival into the twenty-first century is to be assured. I commend each chapter author for his willingness to discuss the delicate issues surrounding the private liberal arts junior college in this country.

Robert H. Woodroof
Editor

Robert H. Woodroof is assistant professor of communication at Pepperdine University, Malibu, California.

Once deemed the answer to the cries for a more egalitarian higher education system in the United States, the private liberal arts junior college is now in its forty-fifth year of decline.

A History of Resilience

Robert H. Woodroof

Several distinctly different types of junior colleges exist in America, each serving a specific constituency. This volume will focus on the private liberal arts junior college (hereafter called *private junior college*), which ushered in the age of the junior college. This resilient, archetypal alternative to traditional higher education began rather quietly in the mid 1800s, reaching its zenith in the mid 1940s.

The private junior college served an important function in the development of higher education in the United States. It entered the higher education scene almost unnoticed in the mid nineteenth century and operated for many years before educational reform began echoing from coast to coast and border to border.

While private junior colleges were clearing a path into the "unsystematized diversity" of higher education during the period from 1850 to 1890, a conflict was brewing that finally reached a heightened pitch in the last decade of the century (Brubacher and Rudy, 1976, p. 405). That conflict, a result of the systematic move toward standardization of curriculum design and degree attainment, concerned the quality of the entire educational system. Education in the United States had already moved from a carbon copy of the European model—that is, "a prescribed and classical curriculum serving young men often from the families of the elite and affluent"—to a system serving a broader cross section of youth in this country (Diener, 1986, pp. 3-4).

But it was a rather undisciplined, unfocused move. The system was becoming largely ineffective in serving an increasingly industrial and urban society (Diener, 1986). There seemed to be a growing need for reform that would offer higher education to more of the public but would still move it toward an elitism that would rival that of the European model. Before a true elite form of higher education could be achieved, however, educational leaders had to address the level of excellence in the lower divisions. This concern initiated the great debate that spawned the junior college.

The Great Debate

Where should the line be drawn between secondary education and college? The entire U.S. system entered the debate, focusing national attention on the thirteenth and fourteenth years of education, commonly known today as the freshman and sophomore years of college. There were many suggestions and even some doubts about whether any line could be drawn. William Rainey Harper recommended three options that could spell new life for a foundering educational system:

1. Strong high schools and academies should be permitted to stretch their offerings to the thirteenth and fourteenth years, thus creating six-year high schools.

2. Weak four-year colleges should drop their junior and senior years and concentrate on the freshman and sophomore years (referred to later as "decapitation").

3. Successful four-year colleges and universities could make a strong move to divide their undergraduate years in half. The first two years (which Harper labeled "academic college" and, later, "junior college") would serve as the true dividing line between lower- and upper-division work; the last two years (which Harper labeled "university college" and, later, "senior college") would serve as the serious preparatory years for graduate study (Brubacher and Rudy, 1976, p. 255).

Harper's ideas proved to be an efficient way to educate increasing numbers of the nation's youth based on their capabilities and career directions. His solutions met with mixed reviews, applauded by some and viewed as improbable or impractical by others. But the idea of dividing upper- and lower-division studies was an enduring one that seemed to take hold quickly. The twenty-year period between 1890 and 1910 became a time for testing Harper's new efficiency. Perhaps the most significant fallout of this flurry of activity was that higher education was preparing itself for the new era of egalitarianism, led ultimately by the junior college.

A new order of education was becoming stronger each year as it began to solve the critical needs of a society increasingly concerned with the education of the masses. The move to raise the level of credibility of the university became a new force for educating the people of the United States. The growing egalitarianism meant a new level of authority among the world's most respected educational systems. The European model was replaced by a strong move toward a new model: the American model of education.

Eventually, as the junior college movement split into two separate systems—community colleges and private junior colleges—education was no longer the privilege of the few but rather the right of everyone. But instead of confirming their place in the nation's higher education system, private junior colleges faced a decline that cut short their brief, bright period of expansion. The rapid rise of the community college and the economic perils of private education began to take their toll.

Expansion and Decline

The historical development of the private junior college spans 136 years, dating back to the 1851 founding of Lasell Female Academy, now operating as Lasell Junior College. There is some disagreement about which college was the first junior college—but a review of the curriculum of Lasell in the 1850s tends to confirm that, even before the term was coined by Harper, this small, single-sex institution was the first private junior college in the country (Wilson, 1939).

However, growth as a result of the national junior college movement really began around 1890 as weak senior colleges began to "decapitate" themselves and strong academies expanded to offer the first two years. The period of expansion and decline, therefore, spans approximately a hundred years. The patterns of expansion show that the numbers of students and institutions increased steadily until they reached a zenith in the mid 1940s.

At that time, three factors began taking their toll on all private junior colleges: the introduction and growing strength of the community college, the demands of World War II, and financial constraints brought on by small enrollments.

The pressure was most acute for the liberal arts sector. By the end of the war in 1945, a visible decline was spreading. Table 1 shows the development of the private junior college from 1890 through 1988, contrasting it to the development of the community college and other public junior colleges. (Note that in 1900 no public community or junior colleges existed.) In only four decades, private junior colleges have dropped 75 percent, from a high of approximately 350 institutions to the current low of 89.

As it became more difficult for the private junior college to remain solvent in the 1940s because of rising costs and competition from the public sector, the surviving colleges rebounded with better marketing plans to boost their enrollments (Sargent, 1959). The result was a reduction in the rate of closures during the fifteen-year period from 1950 to 1965 and an increase of 75 percent in the size of the average fall enrollment compared with 1945.

Table 1. The Historical Development of the Private Junior College—Contrasted with Public Junior College Development

Year	Institutions Private	Institutions Public	Students Private	Students Public	Average Enrollment Private	Average Enrollment Public
1890	7	0	250	0	36	0
1900	27	0	1,000	0	37	0
1920	125	40	5,200	3,000	42	75
1930	258	178	29,000	45,000	112	253
1940	349	261	68,000	168,000	195	644
1950	296	326	104,000	454,000	351	1,394
1960	273	390	95,000	650,000	348	1,859
1970	170	850	75,000	1,950,000	441	2,294
1988	89	1,050	46,720	4,700,000	525	4,476

Source: Data extracted from Eells, 1931; Straughn and Straughn, 1983; *Junior College Journal*, 1930, 1940, 1950.

But the boom did not last. By the 1970s, and especially during the 1974 and 1981 recessions, increased enrollments were the luxury of those few institutions with well-funded and successful recruitment programs. Multiplying expenses brought about by double-digit inflation proved too costly for scores of private junior colleges operating on the edge of disaster.

Some of the colleges decided to gamble with limited financial reserves by reversing the decapitation trend of the early 1900s, adding a junior and senior year and becoming baccalaureate institutions. Others joined forces with stronger nearby senior colleges. But many simply closed their doors, leaving behind a legacy of valiant but futile struggle.

A poignant example of this dilemma occurred during the research process for this volume. While developing a list of those first few junior colleges founded before 1910 that are still in existence today, I phoned Saint Paul's College in Concordia, Missouri, a private junior college founded in 1905 and still operating as late as 1986. The woman who answered the phone stated with the familiarity of a thousand repetitions, "I regret to tell you that Saint Paul's College ceased operations in May 1986."

A search for the seven surviving private junior colleges founded as junior colleges before 1910 ended with a list of only four (two recently had become senior colleges). The results of this research serve as an effective miniature of the history of the rise and decline of the private junior college. The fate of the remaining four junior colleges is very much in question, especially two with enrollments of 103 and 185, respectively.

This brief history of the private junior college serves as a backdrop for the following chapters. Chapters Two through Seven discuss areas important to the survival of the private junior college, with each author expressing a cautious optimism countered by imperatives essential to success. In the final chapter, I tally the strengths and weaknesses of the private junior college and set them against the realities of current trends in higher education. My conclusion is not so much in opposition to the other authors as it is less optimistic. This approach gives you, the reader, the opportunity to determine your own conclusions about the viability of the private liberal arts junior college.

References

Brubacher, J. S., and Rudy, W. *Higher Education in Transition.* New York: Harper & Row, 1976.
Diener, T. *Growth of an American Invention—A Documentary of the Junior and Community College Movement.* New York: Greenwood Press, 1986.
Eells, W. C. *The Junior College.* Boston: Houghton Mifflin, 1931.
Junior College Journal. Selected issues. Washington, D.C.: American Association of Junior Colleges, 1930, 1940, 1950.
Sargent, F. P. *The F. Porter Sargent Series of Promotional Books.* (3rd ed.) Self-published, 1959.
Straughn, C. T., and Straughn, B. L. (eds.). *Lovejoy's College Guide.* (16th ed.) New York: Monarch Press, 1983.
Wilson, T. H. "The First Four-Year Junior College." *Junior College Journal,* 1939, *9,* 361–365.

Robert H. Woodroof is assistant professor of communication, Pepperdine University, Malibu, California.

The private liberal arts junior college is an endangered species. Its survival will depend on a number of saving graces, not the least of which is commitment to the basic values of the higher education system in the United States.

The Private Junior College in Higher Education's Future

Nelson M. Hoffman, Jr.

On first considering the question of whether there is a place for the private junior college in the future of higher education, one is tempted to say, "Of course there is!" But upon more sober reflection, it appears that any conclusion requires some study. Those who have been involved in that area of higher education for many years may not want to think otherwise. On the one hand, the private junior college may be fighting a financial and demographic battle it cannot win; on the other, its ability to offer more students a viable educational option may be making it an institution whose time has come at last. The assumption of this writer is that there is a place for the private junior college in higher education's future and that this place can be assured by careful control and wise governance.

One cannot deny that the private junior college has served an important segment of our society for the past one hundred years or so. Since it is generally a smaller institution than the four-year college, it has appealed to those who may have felt ill at ease in a larger setting; it has attracted those whose intellectual skills may have been hampered by inadequate secondary school training; and it has ordinarily been less expensive than the private four-year college, although more expensive than the public two-year institution since the advent of the community college. The emphasis has usually been on the liberal arts rather than on vocational studies, and many have looked upon the private junior college as an excellent place to more than adequately prepare for the last two years at a baccalaureate institution. Whatever the reason, it has had broad appeal.

The Dominant Sector

There are those of the opinion that the two-year college may dominate postsecondary education for the masses in the future in both the public and private arenas. If this is the case, the private sector must be prepared to assume a more important role in higher education. This optimistic conclusion is based partly on the fact that, because of the national and international economic situation, attendance at most four-year institutions will be beyond the financial means of many well-qualified students. Those not planning to attend a graduate school can receive a solid and complete education in the two-year private liberal arts college, and most can acquire the necessary expertise for a career or paraprofessional position at about half the cost of a four-year college.

Some may argue that such paraprofessional training dilutes the concept of the "liberal arts," but it is obvious that the concept should include the understanding that the primary purpose of obtaining an education is not to gather data and information but to broaden the base of understanding and to learn how to think. Hutchins (1936, p. 33) has written, "There is a conflict between one aim of the university, the pursuit of truth for its own sake, and another which it professes too, the preparation of men and women for their life work. This is not a conflict between education and research. It is a conflict between two kinds of education. Both kinds are found in all parts of a university." The private junior college wishing to continue its valuable contribution to American higher education must keep Hutchins's comment in mind.

The private college in the United States preceded the state-supported and -directed college by more than two centuries and, although public institutions enroll several times as many students as do those in the private sector, privately controlled colleges have consistently been on the frontiers of providing knowledge and preparing leaders to lift the nation's culture.

A Values-Oriented Approach to Education

More than public institutions, private colleges have opportunities to devise creative and dynamic programs with an ethical and moral base to address the deep-rooted and pervasive confusion about values and priorities in American society. Private colleges have the greatest potential for providing opportunities for success and for outlining the requirements of a viable and responsible free society (Howard, 1982). The private junior college must realize this responsibility and act accordingly.

Bowen (1982, pp. 132–133) indicated that although there are no time-tested recipes by which colleges may achieve social responsibility, current literature suggests that "higher education does in fact influence moderately the values of its students and that the effects are on the whole consistent with widely accepted goals of education. . . . One may draw the inference that educators had better be concerned about the kind of influence they are exerting and about the kind of influence they ought to be exerting. Neglect of values may be one way of influencing them. It may be a signal that values are unimportant."

Bowen is of the opinion that, for the college, the task of influencing the values of students is eminently worth attempting and that it is of vital importance to society that it be attempted. The private junior college is in a unique position to play an increasingly important role with regard to the teaching of values if it will give sufficient thought and resources to the proper and most rewarding way of accomplishing the task.

The Association of American Colleges (1975) contends that private higher education is an important, if not indispensable, part of the American higher education system. It adds diversity, offers competition to an otherwise all-embracing public system, provides a center of academic freedom removed from political influence, is deeply committed to liberal learning, is concerned for human and individual personality, sets standards, provides educational leadership, and saves the taxpayers money.

The High Cost of Education

Nothing, it would seem, is of greater immediate concern to educators and students than the costs involved, costs that seem to be increasing at an alarming rate every year. Dickmeyer (1982) suggests that tuition setting is the key to the success or failure of the small, private junior college, since most such institutions are heavily tuition dependent. Tuition accounts for an average of 55 percent of the educational and general budget in private colleges, meaning that enrollment levels—usually dictated by tuition rates—are critical to the college's financial health.

Compounding the problem is that private junior colleges must compete with all those in the public sector for qualified faculty members, who generally are interested in positions with higher salaries. Fortunately, some highly dedicated professors will accept lower salaries in order to teach students in a private junior college. They have, it would seem, almost a missionary interest in working with young people in a situation where the quality of the student and the institution is more important than financial remuneration. The junior college that can appeal to such qualified people is indeed fortunate.

The private junior college will continue to have financial difficulties in the years to come unless it has such a large endowment that tuition income is of little importance. According to a 1987 study by the National Institute of Independent Colleges and Universities (NIICU), private colleges in the 1983-84 academic year received an average of 6.4 percent of their total income from endowments and 11.4 percent from gifts, or a total of 17.8 percent from both sources. Public institutions received 3.8 percent of their income in these ways—but they also received 62 percent from state and federal funds, while private colleges averaged just 17.8 percent from state and federal governments. More significantly, while private colleges received 55 percent of their income from tuition, public institutions received only 16.1 percent in that manner.

Furthermore, according to the NIICU report, the private college student and his or her family pay 65 percent of the total cost of education, with 12 percent of the balance coming from federal loans, 10 percent from college financial aid, 5 percent from federal grants, 5 percent from state grants, and 2 percent from federal College Work-Study programs. Therefore, only 35 percent of the cost for an average student to attend a private college comes from other than his or her own personal resources. The major point here is that future sources of income for public institutions will likely remain nearly the same, while state and federal aid to the private sector, for both the college and the individual family, may decrease.

A question that should be under constant consideration at private junior colleges is whether the school could continue to operate if *all* state and federal funds were to disappear. The private junior college that wishes to retain the appellation of "private" has no good reason to expect *any* additional public funds for itself, and grants and loans to students attending these colleges may also someday disappear. The wise board of trustees of the private junior college would do well to prepare a contingency plan.

Another continuing concern to all involved in higher education is that many students who attend private colleges are graduating with heavy personal debts that will take many years to repay. Brademas (1982), president of New York University, is of the opinion that students who are forced to pay much more for their education are increasingly likely to choose fields of study solely on the basis of promise of future financial security. Where, Brademas asks, will philosophers, musicians, and teachers come from? Where will we find our humanists and public servants? Private colleges, he goes on to say, are heavily dependent on tuition for income and especially endangered by reduction in student aid. Twenty years ago, 50 percent of all college students were enrolled in private institutions. Today the figure is only one in five.

Mayhew (1979) suggests that certain colleges may not be able to make it through the 1980s because of financial problems; he cites as particularly vulnerable the private single-sex junior college. For the balance of the twentieth century, it would seem likely that students from average-income families wishing to go to private colleges will choose institutions where the cost is reasonable and from which they will not emerge with heavy debts. This is another argument in favor of the private junior college, where the student can graduate in two years with a valid degree in the liberal arts and a paraprofessional readiness but, in many instances, with less than half the debt incurred at a private four-year college.

Enrollment Concerns

In addition to financial problems, the private junior college faces, as do all colleges, the matter of a potential enrollment decline. Although many prognosticators were of the opinion that enrollments would have been curtailed sharply in private institutions by the later years of this decade, most colleges are reporting an increase in applications and admissions, however slight. Although the chances of the enrollment decline would appear to be greater for two-year private colleges, such institutions believe their salvation lies in the intangibles: loyal alumni who are willing, it is hoped, to send their sons and daughters; continued support resulting from church affiliation; and the general goodwill of their communities.

The fears of lower enrollments are generated by statistics showing an average of four million eighteen-year-olds in the country each year in the early 1980s, with indications of a drop in that figure for later in the decade. About two-thirds of these graduated from high school, with only about 15 percent going on to private colleges (NIICU, 1987).

It would appear that, in spite of costs, more of these high school graduates are deciding to go to college, a result, perhaps, of more aggressive recruitment and marketing on the part of college admissions officers, coupled with the increasing realization that to be completely educated one must have a college degree.

Additionally, more nontraditional students—those who have delayed their college entrance for a few years—are registering for classes, although many are part-time students. This older cohort has become and will continue to be a valuable source of students, and colleges must adapt their programs to meet the needs of these individuals.

According to Hodgkinson (1983), the most rapidly growing job markets in the last decade of this century will be in data processing and computers. The private junior college, wishing to continue to be true to the liberal arts, must find a way to incorporate these new subjects into its curriculum. Since more and more high schools are offering classes in such areas, many more students will bypass college entirely and receive sufficient additional training from their employers. They will be well trained to do the job for which they will have been hired, but, according to Hirsch (1987), they will be "culturally illiterate."

The private junior college will have to be particularly alert to the growing trend of major corporations toward hiring high school graduates and promising an adequate education after employment. Fortunately, there are many businesses currently indicating that they want college graduates who have been well educated in the basic liberal arts. These companies will then provide their employees with additional on-the-job training. Nevertheless, the private junior college must actively recruit those nontraditional students who want to start work on or complete a degree, or who want to refresh themselves in some particular area. Since most such people will enroll on a part-time basis, the college will need to consider the scheduling and facilities necessary to make the college attractive and appealing.

Presidents Are Cautiously Optimistic

The results of a personal sampling of twelve presidents of United Methodist junior colleges indicated that, although the leaders are proud of their graduates who complete their educations with Associate of Arts degrees, they generally see their institutions not as offering primarily the terminal degree but rather as being transition colleges or preparing their graduates for entry into the junior year of a college or university. They see themselves in the position of being able to prepare their students for roles of leadership and responsibility, as well as providing them with opportunities for personal expression.

These presidents believe their institutions are unique, and they are of the opinion that if they stress this uniqueness, they will not only survive but grow. This is especially true, they feel, in their work with the nontraditional student, although they also sense the necessity of being able to provide traditional students with the necessary changes demanded by their communities.

The leaders also believe that, to a certain extent, they are fighting a kind of discrimination based on an erroneous impression on the part of the general public as to what the role of the private junior college is. They need greater visibility for the achievements of successful graduates who may or may not have gone on to senior colleges. To a great extent, they resent the fact that many community colleges are awarding the Associate of Arts degree in addition to their usual Associate of Science and other degrees, because they feel that, in general, the community college has diluted the liberal arts portion of their program. They want to see the reputation of the Associate of Arts degree enhanced and believe that it will be if private junior colleges continue to stress the liberal arts and their important role in higher education.

These private college presidents see their institutions, unlike community colleges, as upholding the standards of a "true" college with liberal arts and paraprofessional offerings, rather than those of a "training" institution, which may not deserve the appellation of "college."

They also see themselves as having the potential to enhance moral and spiritual concepts and provide opportunities for human growth and development, which the community colleges do not have. Since many are residential schools, they also are able, it is felt, to provide a place where learning to live together is part of the educational experience, so important at this crucial stage in the life of the traditional student.

The respondents see the need to continue doing what they have been doing, but in a better fashion. Their uniqueness must continually be emphasized and the liberal arts strictly upheld. Although they see no need for major innovations, they are of the opinion that they may need to adjust to appeal to more nontraditional students while still attempting to maintain adequate admissions standards. Most of them see no possibility and have no desire to become four-year institutions but are quite proud of the role they now play in higher education.

With regard to admissions standards, private junior colleges must not succumb to the temptation to lower their requirements so that they become, in effect, grades thirteen and fourteen. It must become well known that private junior colleges do have respectable admissions standards. The college must also proclaim loudly and clearly its own purpose and mission, and then prove to its constituencies that it should exist, never forgetting to emphasize the importance of examining one's value system as an integral part of learning.

The Import of Pluralism

Small colleges are places where real creativity and innovation occur, where ideas can be tested and possibly institutionalized, according to West (1982). Pluralism is one of the greatest strengths of American higher education, and it is exceedingly important that those who exalt the diversity of higher education understand that small private colleges are an important part of that diversity. The private junior college has the responsibility of seeing that this message is broadcast widely among its own constituents, as well as in the larger geographical arena.

The private junior college will continue to play an important part in the future of higher education in this country if it remembers its own unique and distinctive calling and does not try to expand beyond its capabilities. There is no need for the private college to try to duplicate the offerings of the public college so as to be more able to compete for students. At the time of the Dartmouth College decision (which gave colleges the right to private control), Daniel Webster said, "It will be a dangerous, a most dangerous experiment to hold these institutions subject to the rise and fall of popular parties and the fluctuations of political opinions" (National Commission on United Methodist Higher Education, 1976, p. 54).

Private colleges are among the most visible fruits of a pluralistic society. An independent academic estate is critical to the enhancement of America's diverse cultures and the preservation of personal and group freedom. A strong independent sector can counter the tendency within a state toward homogeneity in purpose and program and the pressures toward merely utilitarian objectives by providing an alternative to a state-controlled monopoly of higher education.

Private colleges contribute toward diversity by their ability to select students, faculty, and trustees in keeping with their stated and functional purposes. Since they are less subject than public institutions to political shifts in areas such as funding, they can maintain their integrity, which tends to strengthen academic freedom for all higher education (NIICU, 1987).

McGrath (1981) believes that few subjects should be of greater concern today, not only to educators but to the public at large, than the preservation of independent colleges and universities. Only through the continuation of their services can the well-being of the public system itself be ensured.

Reaching the Twenty-First Century

In spite of the obvious difficulties facing small, private junior colleges, I believe that most of these institutions will survive and, indeed, thrive during the remainder of the twentieth century. The demise and extinction of a private college is a violent activity and takes place only after many attempts at resuscitation, including hundreds of committee meetings, strategy sessions, compromise attempts, and urgent appeals. Some, at death's doorstep itself, manage to survive and receive new impetus from unexpected sources. According to Hoffman (1983), those that do end their existence probably do so because of inept leadership, fiscal mismanagement, and a lack of vision and planning.

Not only will most private junior colleges survive but their very survival, as McGrath (1981) has pointed out, will help ensure the continuing strength of all of American higher education. As Cater (1982, pp. 46-47) indicated in his inaugural address upon becoming president of Washington College, "small colleges are indeed among the endangered species. Survival can be won by each college distinguishing itself from other small institutions and by demonstrating that the vital signs are more enduring than the predicted death tolls. The pursuit of excellence should be the goal since there is already an excess of competition among the mediocre."

The private junior college has a place in American higher education, but these institutions are going to have to redouble their efforts to see that their mission and purpose is clearly stated and loudly proclaimed before the general public, that they maintain their integrity as educational institutions with curricular substance, that they consciously attempt to instill an appreciation of values and integrity in their students, and that they are aware of the pitfalls that may lie ahead with regard to finances and a potential drop in student enrollments. The private junior college has an important part to play and will be successful if it does so with complete honesty and careful concern for its constituency.

References

Association of American Colleges. *Private Education, First Annual Report.* Washington, D.C.: Association of American Colleges, 1975.
Bowen, H. R. *The State of the Nation and the Agenda for Higher Education.* San Francisco: Jossey-Bass, 1982.
Brademas, J. "Supporting Higher Education on All Fronts." *Educational Record,* Summer 1982, pp. 4-7.
Cater, D. "The Idea of a Small College." *AGB Reports,* November/December 1982, pp. 46-47.
Dickmeyer, N. "Institutional Policies for Student Financial Aid." *Perspectives and Projections.* Public Policy Monograph Series, no. 63. Washington, D.C.: National Institute of Independent Colleges and Universities, September 1982.
Hirsch, E. D., Jr. *Cultural Literacy: What Every American Needs to Know.* Boston: Houghton Mifflin, 1987.
Hodgkinson, H. L. *Guess Who's Coming to College: Your Students in 1990.* Washington, D.C.: National Institute of Independent Colleges and Universities, 1983.
Hoffman, N. M. *The Private Two-Year College: The Present Situation.* An Occasional Paper. Charlottesville, Va.: Southern Association of Community and Junior Colleges, 1983.
Howard, J. A. *Private Higher Education: The Job Ahead.* Vol. 10: *Values in Private Higher Education.* Washington, D.C.: American Association of Presidents of Independent Colleges and Universities, 1982.
Hutchins, R. M. *The Higher Learning in America.* New Haven, Conn.: Yale University Press, 1936.
McGrath, E. J. *Private Higher Education: The Job Ahead.* Vol. 9: *The Independent Institution of Higher Education in the Eighties.* Washington, D.C.: American Association of Presidents of Independent Colleges and Universities, 1981.
Mayhew, L. B. *Surviving the Eighties: Strategies and Procedures for Solving Fiscal and Enrollment Problems.* San Francisco: Jossey-Bass, 1979.
National Commission on United Methodist Higher Education. *A College-Related Church: United Methodist Perspectives.* Nashville, Tenn.: National Commission on United Methodist Higher Education, 1976.
National Institute of Independent Colleges and Universities. *The Truth About Costs in the Independent Sector of Higher Education.* Washington, D.C.: National Institute of Independent Colleges and Universities, 1987.
West, D. C. "How Endangered Are Small Colleges?" *Educational Record,* Fall 1982, pp. 14-17.

Nelson M. Hoffman, Jr., is president emeritus of Midway College, Midway, Kentucky.

Because survival is a question mark for the private junior college, this unique segment of higher education must adopt sound marketing strategies based on rigorous self-study and modern consumer behavior trends.

A Professional Approach to Marketing the Private Junior College

Peter T. Mitchell

As higher education entered the decade of the 1980s, colleges and universities looked to business and industry for models and methods to achieve stability and to exhibit accountability. Projected declining enrollments and potential retrenchment compelled institutions to seek solutions for potential decline. Higher education began viewing itself as a complex service industry in need of modern management techniques. Perhaps the best evidence of this shift in philosophy of leadership toward a business model is found in the adoption of marketing concepts.

The idea of marketing is not new, but its adoption in higher education has been remarkably swift. In conversations among admissions officers, academic deans, deans of students, provosts, and presidents, concepts like segmentation, targeting, and positioning are becoming commonly understood.

Incorporating marketing into the administration of colleges and universities did meet with some resistance. During the late 1970s and early 1980s, many administrators and most faculty equated marketing only with promotion, advertising, and public relations. This limited vision precipitated a growing sentiment against marketing in academia and a fear that the emerging Madison Avenue attitude might replace sensible admissions counseling.

This initial marketing backlash was the result of inappropriate and overly slick promotional activity on the part of some institutions. However, the combination of time constraints, pressing need, and competition compelled colleges and universities to examine more seriously the potential of developing marketing strategies. A few innovative colleges and universities, representative of all major institutional types, have demonstrated how a comprehensive marketing strategy could improve higher education in general and enhance specific institutions that advocate its precepts. Moreover, as the pool of high school graduates dwindled and the competition for students intensified, marketing was perceived less as hucksterism and more as a creative tool to ensure institutional survival.

Of all segments of higher education, the private two-year college is most susceptible to the "promises" of marketing. Because of their small size, limited enrollment, dependence on tuition revenues, and financial vulnerability, independent junior colleges feel the enrollment squeeze before most larger colleges and universities do. Yet an unwillingness to be complacent about recruitment efforts, coupled with a survival-level need to experiment with new techniques, has compelled many junior colleges to view marketing as a viable—even necessary—strategy for administration. For these volatile institutions, marketing has become a strategy appropriate to their unique characteristics, financial resources, and uncertain future.

Comprehensive marketing compels private junior colleges to ask focusing questions repeatedly: What business are we in? What markets do we serve? How can we preserve our mission in a cost-effective manner? Stripped of its sophisticated techniques and intricate strategic considerations, the marketing approach still offers the private two-year college that crucial element of focus on function. Marketing begins with asking questions that force junior colleges to take an honest and detailed look at themselves and the type of student they serve. Among the myriad benefits obtained through a comprehensive marketing strategy are the following:

- The ability to restate or reaffirm the mission of the college on the basis of a meticulous examination of the institution's own strengths and weaknesses
- Analysis of students' wants and needs and, as a result, a more responsive institution
- Design of promotional materials that reflect both institutional strengths and prospective students' interests
- Evaluation of each recruitment technique, to determine which ones are producing positive results at what cost
- The consistency to be gained by working toward specific, realistic objectives and enrollment goals
- Steady improvement, achieved by using a master strategy with yearly updates and revisions.

Despite limited resources, the independent two-year college has adopted the philosophical underpinnings of a marketing strategy for management. Small size, shared values, and a common understanding of institutional mission and purpose are not only key attributes of the private junior college but also pivotal elements for a marketing strategy necessary for internalization. Moreover, faculty and administrators at private junior colleges tend to associate themselves more with institutional purpose than with the goals of a single discipline or department. Consequently, faced with adversity in recruitment, the entire junior college community could accept the marketing strategy enthusiastically.

Once an institution has accepted the basic premises of marketing, energies should be channeled toward designing an appropriate and effective strategy. This strategy should include research into the institution, its mission, and the public's perception of it. The junior college then undertakes a careful planning of its academic offerings, its enrollment goals, its promotional literature, and its recruitment practices. The purpose of an effective marketing strategy is to target the message of the institution to those prospective students who would match most clearly the goals and "personality" of the junior college.

A Marketing Model for Private Junior Colleges

Although the basic tenets of marketing seem obvious enough, the concept should be sophisticated and systematic when implemented. A typical marketing model incorporates six functions: research, product development, strategy formulation, promotion, communication, and review components (Barton, 1978). "What is required, too," according to Barton (1978, p. 33), "is an understanding of the sequential nature of the marketing process—from research, strategy considerations, and decisions on techniques, to implementation, communication, and ongoing evaluation."

In an effort to capture the evolution of the marketing concept within private junior colleges, I have developed, refined, and revised an admissions marketing model for independent two-year colleges. Conceived in 1980, the model was revised and presented to presidents of independent two-year colleges on December 7, 1987, at a conference jointly sponsored by the National Council of Independent Junior Colleges (NCIJC) and the National Association of Independent Colleges and Universities (NAICU). An awareness of the unique aspects of the private junior college guided the model development process.

There are four main components in the model: research, product development, promotion strategies, and evaluation. Each component is subdivided into areas of responsibility that must be accepted to fulfill that component. Finally, each area of responsibility is broken down into specific tasks and activities. The model moves from general to specific, from theory to practice, from responsibility to task (see Figure 1 and Exhibit 1).

Research Component. Before an institution can embark on a master marketing strategy, it must collect and interpret important information about itself, its students, and its competition. The data gathered provide the basis for making decisions about the product and its promotion. Adequate research lays the groundwork for the model and the entire marketing management process (Adler, 1977; Barton, 1978; Kotler, 1975).

The logical place to begin is to evaluate what is most easily understood. Consequently, the initial research should be directed at an *analysis of the institution* (Johnson, 1979). Examination of any mission, goal, or purpose statement provides the framework for understanding an overview of the college. The mission statement can be the essence of the institution, the image it desires to project to all external publics.

Once the overview is accomplished, it is important to assess *the financial condition,* since the ability to invest in product or promotional development depends on adequate financial backing. The personnel resources must be inventoried to discover the strength of this labor-intensive, people-oriented service industry.

Along the same lines, an assessment of specific physical and plant resources produces a list of attractive or unattractive features or accommodations to present to prospective students. Several offices throughout the campus must be tapped for *historical information* that will enable the college to develop a perspective including its significant past accomplishments. *Attrition studies* help in understanding some of the problems between student expectations and delivery of services.

This institutional analysis should result in an honest and objective profile of the college. It should also point to the potential for implementing a marketing strategy. If the institution is afraid or reluctant to undergo self-examination, the idea of marketing will be only rhetoric. Conversely, open institutions will consider new techniques to achieve success. Success demands that this assessment project the institution as it is and not as it would like to be.

Once an institution understands itself, it then must begin to analyze the students it serves (Ihlanfeldt, 1980; Sullivan and Litten, 1976). This student analysis should focus first on enrolled students and their characteristics. Much of the necessary data is contained in high school transcripts, admissions applications, and national test score reports. High school grade point average, rank in class, socioeconomic background, career goals, hobbies, interests, and extracurricular activities are integrated into a profile of the type of student served by a particular college.

Likewise, it is important to compare enrolled students with accepted applicants who did not enroll. Discovering why students did not enroll

Figure 1. Two-Year Independent College Admission Marketing Model

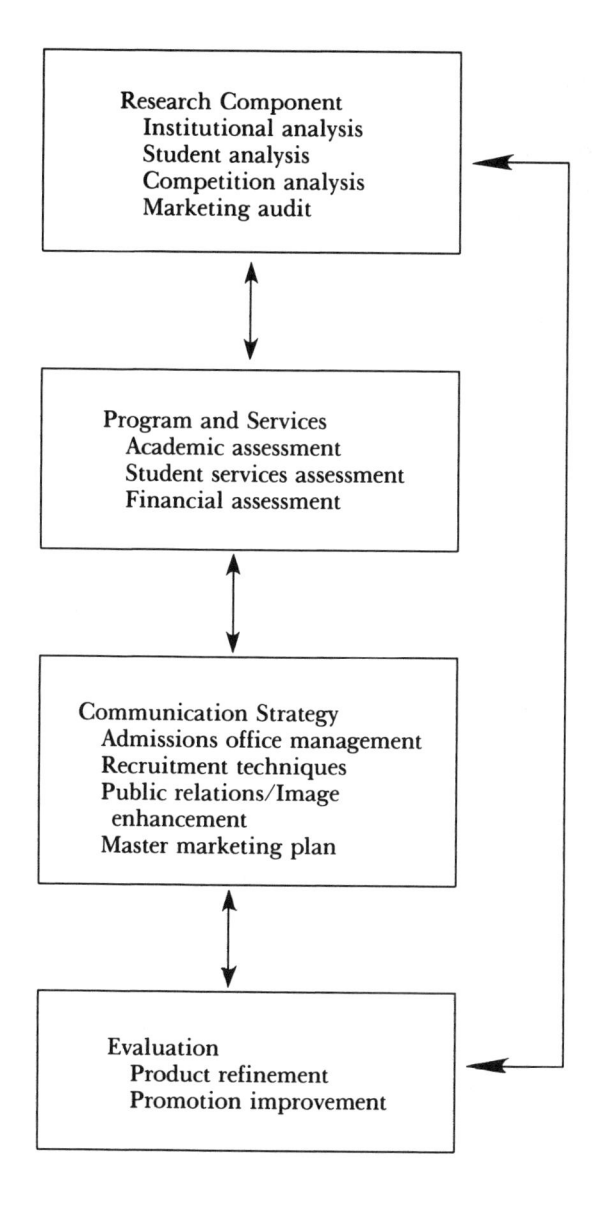

```
┌─────────────────────────────────┐
│   Research Component            │
│      Institutional analysis     │◄──┐
│      Student analysis           │   │
│      Competition analysis       │   │
│      Marketing audit            │   │
└─────────────────────────────────┘   │
              ▲▼                      │
┌─────────────────────────────────┐   │
│   Program and Services          │   │
│      Academic assessment        │   │
│      Student services assessment│   │
│      Financial assessment       │   │
└─────────────────────────────────┘   │
              ▲▼                      │
┌─────────────────────────────────┐   │
│   Communication Strategy        │   │
│      Admissions office management│  │
│      Recruitment techniques     │   │
│      Public relations/Image     │   │
│        enhancement              │   │
│      Master marketing plan      │   │
└─────────────────────────────────┘   │
              ▲▼                      │
┌─────────────────────────────────┐   │
│   Evaluation                    │   │
│      Product refinement         │◄──┘
│      Promotion improvement      │
└─────────────────────────────────┘
```

Exhibit 1. Marketing Model Components

I. Research
   A. Institutional Analysis
      1. Mission/goals/purpose
      2. Historical narrative
      3. Financial status
      4. Personnel resources
      5. Potential for marketing
   B. Student Analysis
      1. Inquiries
      2. Applicants
         a. Enrolled
         b. Nonmatriculating
      3. Markets
         a. Established
         b. New/experimental
      4. Student decision making
         a. The process
         b. Key influencers
   C. Competitive Analysis
      1. Private colleges
      2. Public colleges
      3. Noncollegiate experiences
      4. Position map
   D. Marketing Audit
      1. Identify marketing activities
      2. Evaluate their effectiveness
II. Program and Services
   A. Academic Assessment
      1. Employment needs and trends
      2. Career preparation
      3. Transfer articulation
      4. Faculty evaluation
      5. Program-of-study reviews
   B. Student Services Assessment
      1. Residential life
      2. Counseling
      3. Student activities
      4. Extracurricular activities
      5. Health services
      6. Placement
   C. Financial Assessment
      1. Tuition and fees
      2. Room and board
      3. Financial aid
      4. Price-packaging strategy
III. Communication Strategy
   A. Admissions Office Management
      1. Goals and objectives
      2. Duties/responsibilities

Exhibit 1. *(continued)*

      3. Systematic treatment
         a. Inquiries
         b. Applicants
      4. Staff training
         a. Marketing
         b. Selling/counseling
   B. Recruitment Techniques
      1. Communications
         a. Publications
         b. Advertising
         c. Counseling
         d. Presentations
      2. Recruitment events
         a. On campus
         b. Off campus
   C. Public Relations
      1. Image enhancement
      2. Positioning
   D. Master Marketing Plan
      1. Research
      2. Design
      3. Implementation
IV. Evaluation
   A. Product Refinement
      1. Advisory councils
      2. Accreditation self-studies
      3. Alumni surveys
      4. Enrolled-student feedback
      5. Market research
   B. Promotion Improvement
      1. Activity evaluation
      2. Publications evaluation
      3. Cost-benefit analysis of advertising
      4. Enrolled-student focus-group interviews
      5. Comparison of conversion rates

can provide clues to areas that need strengthening within the institution or the admissions office. Evaluating inquiries to determine how applicants first heard about the college enables an institution to segment its market and target its message. Finally, junior colleges must examine their established markets (such as local high school seniors within commuting distance, feeder high schools for dormitory students, and children of alumni), as well as prospective new markets for student enrollment (such as adults interested in continuing education, industrial training or retraining, and personal enrichment). Looking into the marketplace can lead to new ideas for avenues of service.

    The self-study achieved through institutional and student analyses compels an institution to *look outward toward its competition*. This analysis should include private two-year and four-year colleges, community colleges, and state colleges, as well as noneducational alternatives, such as work, marriage, or the military, that are available to potential students.

An understanding of the full dimension of competitive forces could lead to beginning efforts toward *positioning the junior college* in relation to other colleges and universities. Competitive evaluations should survey promotional materials for these other institutions and utilize both interviews with enrolled students who had explored these alternatives and on-site visits. Just as the tendency persists to make false assumptions about one's own institution, based on insufficient or erroneous information, it is also wise to be wary of false generalizations about the competition.

Product Development Component. Once an institution has thoroughly analyzed its strengths and weaknesses, its students, and its competition, it must use this information to improve curricular and cocurricular activities (that is, its products and services). Product refinements and improvements in services will become increasingly important in the face of rapidly escalating competition for a dramatically declining pool of traditional college-age youth.

At the core of any college are its academic programs of study. Careful scrutiny of each program, course, and teaching style should be a continuous, high-priority administrative process (Kotler, 1976). For a private junior college specializing in career-oriented programs, an academic assessment tends to emphasize success in the job market. An evaluation of local employment needs and economic trends can provide important information for curriculum planning. The theme of career preparation can dictate course content and even teaching styles. Because transfer into senior colleges or universities is the other emphasis of the private two-year college, efforts to maintain regional accreditation, to strengthen liberal arts courses, and to facilitate transfer articulation should be central.

Although academic offerings are the raison d'être for the existence of a college, these institutions must not lose sight of their student services (Ihlanfeldt, 1980). Because of small size, private junior colleges accentuate the personal touch in their educational packages. To substantiate this claim, they need a meaningful residential-life program, effective counseling, dependable health services, appropriate extracurricular organizations, interesting student activities, and successful placement for graduates. As the decision-making process of college choice becomes more sophisticated, the student services area will receive more detailed evaluation by prospective students.

In opening up new opportunities and markets, private junior colleges are offering remedial or skill-development courses as well as learning centers and academic support services to educate students who are underprepared for college work, or those from disadvantaged environments. Ideally, student services should play a complementary and supportive role in augmenting the academic programs.

Promotion Strategy Component. Now that the product has been clearly defined, it becomes the responsibility of the admissions office to promote that product. The key to a successful promotion strategy lies within the management of the admissions office (Campbell, 1978; LaBaugh, 1978). The management style adopted should stress goals and objectives. Most admissions operations need the guidance and focus that results from a goal orientation and the setting of objectives. To maximize results, each member of the admissions team should delineate his or her duties and responsibilities.

A crucial aspect of office management is designing a method to communicate effectively with all prospects. A systematic procedure for responding to inquiries and applicants must be established, to ensure prompt and consistent follow-up or "courting" of all prospective students.

With organized and operational office management, the admissions office can begin planning recruitment techniques to achieve enrollment goals. Promotional communications, such as publications, advertising, and direct counseling, should have specific goals and objectives to accomplish. For example, a view book or brochure should elicit an application, a request for more information, or an appointment to visit the campus. Establishing measurable goals forces these sometimes vague promotional pieces to be clear, crisp, and effective. Likewise, each off-campus or on-campus special event should have a clear purpose, and promoters should be able to measure its success.

Shaping activities toward desired outcomes should result in better organized and more productive recruitment techniques. Even public relations should be orchestrated in such a way as to project the desired image of the institution (Geltzer and Reis, 1976). Public relations efforts include sending out news releases, producing alumni publications, and hosting lecture/concert series and community events on campus. Although the effects of these efforts are difficult to measure, more colleges and universities should heed the examples of business and industry in the judicious use of public relations to improve reputation and prestige.

The culmination of effective admissions office management and productive recruitment techniques is the development of a master plan. This master plan becomes the planning document for the entire year. Putting the marketing strategy in writing forces admissions offices to exercise advanced planning, organizes all personnel around a central purpose and method of achieving agreed-upon goals, points to areas that are conspicuously absent from the plan and need improvement, provides built-in evaluation measures, and communicates to the rest of the college that Admissions "has its act together" and is prepared for the challenges of enrollment planning and forecasting. The master plan should include research, design, and estimated costs for implementation that will be necessary to achieve desired goals.

Private junior colleges must force themselves to take time from their busy schedules for short- and long-range planning. Until an admissions office stops to plan and become organized, it will continue to function at a crisis level, always reacting and never controlling its own destiny. This hectic pace creates anxiety, frustration, and lack of fulfillment in the staff. Careful and realistic planning should improve morale as well as enrollment statistics.

Evaluation Component. No admissions marketing model could survive without an evaluation component. Since research plays such a crucial part in the marketing process, a formalized method of evaluation is required (Barton and Treadwell, 1978). This evaluation should lead to product refinement and promotion improvement. Without this component, the model lacks continuity and the ability to be self-perpetuating. Moreover, as competition increases and prospective students become more discerning, new and creative methods to enhance the admissions function will be a necessity for survival.

One positive outgrowth of evaluation should be the discovery of information that will refine or alter the product or services of the college. Certain techniques can facilitate this discovery process. Advisory councils for each major program of study or academic department can serve as barometers of economic or social trends that will affect curricula. These business leaders are in a position to gauge employment needs and specific required skills. Their advice is valuable in planning course content and career counseling or placement services.

Accreditation self-studies contain a wealth of specific and even critical information about the college, prepared by individuals representing every major internal segment of the institution. Moreover, recommendations of the visiting accrediting team provide perspective for future growth and development.

The admissions office also needs to be attuned to the ideas of alumni and currently enrolled students. Focus-group interviews and questionnaires elicit constructive information, coming directly from the "customer" or "user" of the services. Market research efforts are difficult to initiate but are nevertheless powerful tools for product refinement.

Improvement of the promotional strategy is the second advantage of evaluation. Evaluation forms are needed for each on-campus or off-campus activity, public relations event, college presentation, promotional brochure, and advertisement. This evaluation form not only provides an opportunity to measure effectiveness but also directs and monitors the design and development of these recruitment techniques. Knowing in advance what will be the means of measurement guides the creation of the activity, event, or literature.

Measuring the impact of advertising requires (1) a way of tracing inquiries and (2) the actual record-keeping capacity to trace an inquiry through the application stage. In this way, it is possible to conduct a cost-benefit analysis to determine which advertising approach delivered the inquiries that eventually generated enrollments. Again, focus interviews with students, and questionnaires from nonmatriculating accepted applicants, can highlight strengths and weaknesses of promotional techniques, suggest new ideas for promotion improvement, and provide insights into the college choice process (Engledow and Anderson, 1978; Huddleston, 1976).

It is important to compare the rates of inquiries that become applications as well as applicants who become enrolled students because these ratios can point to specific elements of the strategy that warrant immediate attention. If conversion of inquiries to applications is down, then the promotional literature, campus visit structure, and image of the institution are not convincing students to apply. Low conversion rates from applicant to enrolled student often indicate that follow-up has failed to effectively close the sale or that the product or personal recruitment is unsatisfactory or second-rate.

Finally, all this evaluation must result in modifications, additions, and deletions in the master plan. Evaluation carries with it the obligation to use the results to improve the college and its recruitment effort.

This admissions marketing model uses sources of information common to any junior college. Often the best resources are currently enrolled students, faculty, and administrators. Structured interviews or even casual conversations can provide relevant data and constructive insights. Much information can be gleaned from applications, health forms, and other self-report inventories. Accreditation self-studies provide significant information about an institution because they involve the entire college community in a critical evaluation of strengths and weaknesses.

Another resource often overlooked is the community leader. Key people serving on advisory councils and other committees can provide an honest appraisal of community attitudes toward the college. Again, the focus on function, which is so much a part of marketing, surfaces with demanding questions: What business are we in? Whom should we serve? How can we be more effective and efficient?

Three Trends That Affect Marketing Success

Discussions among independent two-year college presidents at NCIJC meetings have identified three trends that will affect the marketing of private junior colleges.

The Need for More Sophisticated Marketing Techniques. Despite the problem of limited resources plaguing most private junior colleges, accepting a marketing approach to admissions carries with it the subsequent responsibility of understanding and utilizing the totality of nonprofit marketing. Although adequate for the early stages of marketing management, the proposed model can be transformed from its present recruitment plan to a true marketing plan only with the inclusion of segmentation, marketing mix, and an in-depth analysis of the external environment. Likewise, substantive marketing functions, such as pricing, product differentiation, positioning, and the process of choosing a college, must be integrated into the total marketing concept.

The Need for "Differentiation." If private junior colleges are to survive the next decade, they must design and implement a strategy that differentiates them from other colleges and universities. Perhaps the single most pressing problem is justifying the high cost of attending a private junior college, despite the negative presumptions concerning the quality of two-year colleges. The competition with the public community college has existed since its inception and has intensified in recent years, with pricing and cost considerations becoming even more important.

Many perceive low-cost (sometimes free) community colleges as similar to independent two-year colleges. Both types of institutions confer associate degrees, have liberal if not open admissions standards, and cater to the student who wants to begin higher education with only two years. Unfortunately, the very term *junior college* connotes secondary quality and status. The problem of cost and quality must be resolved if private junior colleges are to survive the next decade.

Effective marketing management provides one solution to this problem. A marketing master plan would include a specific strategy that responds directly to the price/quality issue. The strategy would contain detailed tactics to change negative perceptions about private junior colleges, to differentiate the private from the public two-year college on attributes other than cost, and to build a convincing case for the positioning of the private junior college as a viable, rewarding, and prestigious alternative to other types of higher education institutions.

Effecting a major shift in public perception and positioning is beyond the scope of an individual institution. An effort of this magnitude requires the support and cooperation of all private two-year colleges. These institutions must pool resources and reduce overt competition with one another in order to mount a unified public relations effort to overcome their major common problem: lack of identity for the private two-year college. Such a movement is developing among NCIJC member colleges.

The Need for Innovation. The third trend is a corollary to the first two and actually highlights the distinct, even unique, attributes of almost all independent two-year colleges. The advantage of small size, a common mission, and shared values is the ability to be responsive to new opportunities as well as to create a sense of community. Small, responsive, and unified organizations are ideal for innovation. The pioneer and the entrepreneur played important roles in the history of the private junior college, and these qualities of adventurousness must be revitalized. In a student market that is changing rapidly and profoundly, institutional flexibility, responsiveness, and willingness to take risks will become increasingly important.

Rather than bemoaning their fate and commiserating over the problems confronting vulnerable private two-year colleges, many institutions are becoming more proactive and more decisive in carving out a niche in higher education. Regardless of the industry, there is always a place for creative and innovative organizations. For a long time, the public community college played the role of innovator, especially in terms of instructional strategies that accommodate alternative learning styles. However, in their quest to be more respected in the higher education system, the community colleges seem to be abandoning that experimental focus. Many large public and private colleges and universities have structures and decision-making processes that are cumbersome and unable to respond to rapid changes in the environment.

In the absence of any key player assuming a more entrepreneurial role, this void creates an ideal opportunity for the private junior college. Whether it concerns designing strategies for teaching traditional liberal arts programs or developing career programs for jobs that may not exist for another year or two, a professional approach to marketing, with its focus on function, would dictate that private junior colleges explore this role as entrepreneur and innovator in higher education.

Conclusion

The future outlook for independent two-year colleges is somewhere between cautiously optimistic and perilous. Those institutions that have internalized a professional approach to marketing will survive and even prosper in the difficult times ahead. Their clarity of purpose, awareness of strengths and weaknesses, and commitment to serving students during the first two years of college augur well in the face of problems and adversity. Unified efforts to articulate the distinct, even unique, attributes of a private junior college also hold promise for all such institutions.

The special challenges resulting from careful scrutiny will extract an added dimension of relevance and responsiveness to student needs from those junior colleges committed to a professional marketing approach. Finally, with renewed confidence and entrepreneurial zest, aggressive, independent two-year colleges will carve out their distinct niche in the complex and diverse industry known as higher education.

References

Adler, L. "Systems Approach to Marketing." In B. Enis and K. Cox (eds.), *Marketing Classics*. (3rd ed.) Newton, Mass.: Allyn & Bacon, 1977.

Barton, D. W., Jr. "Marketing: A Consultant's Evaluation of What Colleges Are Doing." *College and University*, 1978, *53* (4), 557-562.

Barton, D. W., Jr., and Treadwell, D. R., Jr. "Marketing: A Synthesis of Institutional Soul-Searching and Aggressiveness." In D. Barton, Jr., (ed.), *Marketing Higher Education*. New Directions for Higher Education, no. 21. San Francisco: Jossey-Bass, 1978.

Campbell, C. C. "The Administration of Admissions." In D. Barton, Jr., (ed.), *Marketing Higher Education*. New Directions for Higher Education, no. 21. San Francisco: Jossey-Bass, 1978.

Engledow, J. L., and Anderson, R. D. "Putting the Small College Admissions in a Marketing Mode." *College and University*, 1978, *54*, 5-20.

Geltzer, H., and Reis, A. "The Positioning Era: Marketing Strategy for College Admissions in the 1980s." In *A Role for Marketing in College Admissions*. New York: College Entrance Examination Board, 1976.

Huddleston, T. "Marketing: The Applicant Questionnaire." *College and University*, 1976, *51* (2), 214-219.

Ihlanfeldt, W. *Achieving Optimal Enrollments and Tuition Revenues: A Guide to Modern Methods of Market Research, Student Recruitment, and Institutional Pricing*. San Francisco: Jossey-Bass, 1980.

Johnson, D. L. "The Researcher and Nonprofit Marketing: Is Anyone Listening?" In J. Lucas (ed.), *Developing a Total Marketing Plan*. New Directions for Institutional Research, no. 21. San Francisco: Jossey-Bass, 1979.

Kotler, P. *Marketing for Nonprofit Organizations*. Englewood Cliffs, N.J.: Prentice-Hall, 1975.

Kotler, P. "Applying Marketing Theory to College Admissions." In *A Role for Marketing in College Admissions*. New York: College Entrance Examination Board, 1976.

LaBaugh, T. "All Marketing, No Management Make Jack a Dull Director." *National ACAC Journal*, 1978, *21* (4), 24-27.

Sullivan, D. F., and Litten, L. H. "Using Research in Analyzing Student Markets: A Case Study." In *A Role for Marketing in College Admissions*. New York: College Entrance Examination Board, 1976.

Peter T. Mitchell is former president of Lasell Junior College, Newton, Massachusetts.

The modern college curriculum has been labeled irrelevant, fragmented, unfocused, and ineffective. Value-added assessment is one way of proving the success or failure of our academic enterprises. But the cost of such assessment can be prohibitive for the private junior college.

Assessment, the Affordable Way

John H. Williams

"Do not expect what you do not inspect" has become the unofficial watchword of higher education in the last years of the 1980s. In the *Federal Register* of September 8, 1987, the Department of Education published a proposal to change its regulations for recognition of accrediting agencies. Foremost among these changes is a call for greater emphasis on assessment in the accreditation process.

As more and more accrediting agencies begin requiring colleges and universities to have a systematic plan for measuring and documenting the value they add to a student's life, accountability quietly becomes indispensable to the task of higher education. If assessment is so vital, a skeptic might wonder, why hasn't it been done for the last thirty years? Why all the rush now to attend seminars, establish consortia, train staff, and develop techniques for assessment?

Doubts About Past Methods of Assessment

Colleges have always tested students. What is new is doubt—doubt about the validity and reliability of past methods as they are applied in today's academic context. For decades, the final grades a student received from a variety of professors in a wide range of disciplines were believed to be an adequate measure of learning. But charges of grade inflation during the 1970s climaxed in the revelation that teachers did not always use grades to communicate how much a student had learned.

Some faculty members had been using grades to build student self-esteem. Some used them to recruit majors, realizing that good grades encourage students and bad grades frustrate them. Others decided to grade students not according to a professional standard of the knowledge or skills a student ought to have but on the basis of how the student performed compared to the other students in the class. Still others let activities substitute for results by giving bonus points for class attendance, participation in class discussion, or good behavior.

Influential people began to doubt that grade point averages had much to do with what or how much students had actually learned. They wanted independent verification—that is, evaluation from a source other than the instructor. Furthermore, they wanted evidence that the broader claims colleges make about student development have substance. Do students really become more altruistic, better adjusted socially, and more effective as leaders as a result of the total college experience? When outsiders began to ask such questions of colleges, assessment became an administrative as well as a faculty responsibility, and administrators began asking questions.

Core Curriculum, General Education, Retained Knowledge

Before attempting to address any of those questions, distinctions in three areas are in order: core curriculum, general education, and retained knowledge.

Core Curriculum. The core curriculum is a means used to achieve the goal of general education—an education that most agree is necessary and all agree is difficult to define precisely. The majority of American colleges are multilevel schools. They offer instruction in elementary arithmetic, basic reading skills, and the rudiments of composition. They do so because large numbers of students require this instruction if they are to have any hope of graduating. These weaker students hold high school diplomas, but, as they prove, passing grades do not always translate into a credible general education.

To meet the needs of an unequally prepared market, colleges offer a smorgasbord of classes that all, whether easy or demanding, satisfy the requirements of the core curriculum. Some freshmen study calculus; others study arithmetic or basic algebra. Some study engineering physics, some "Physics for Society." Some sophomores study English literature, some "Business Writing." The true "core," or common curriculum, is usually a very limited set of classes, and the general education that undergraduates receive is highly disparate.

General Education. The practical purpose of the core curriculum is not so much to provide a broader or richer academic common ground as to confirm and consolidate the student's secondary education; that is, it ensures a basic general education rather than an extensive general education. The science and mathematics courses highly prepared students take to fulfill general education requirements in college are often easier than the courses they took in high school. Even today, it is entirely conceivable that a talented eighth grader could pass most locally developed "rising junior" tests in English composition and mathematics. These tests serve as obstacles to the incompetent but not as assessments of "higher education." "A horse that can count to ten," said Dr. Johnson, "is a remarkable horse, not a remarkable mathematician." Passing a test on the rudiments of mathematics or composition doesn't prove much either, but at least it sets the floor from which the ceiling may be viewed.

Retained Knowledge. Retained knowledge is what a highly educated person actually retains ten years later from a general college education. In his recent book *Cultural Literacy*, Hirsch (1987, p. 127) writes that "the information that literate people dependably share is extensive but limited." Outside their specialties, college graduates retain a host of impressions and dim recollections, but precious little in the way of detail. For example, many people know that the quadratic formula exists, but how many can write it correctly in the margin of this book? What is the conjugation of a French or Spanish verb in the imperfect tense? How often has the typical person been called upon to use either area of knowledge since college? The virtue of much general education, it appears, is that the student is exposed to and becomes vaguely familiar with many subjects, not that he or she will retain a great deal of detail. Skills or knowledge thoroughly acquired are few; basically, they are those gained in secondary school by dint of endless practice and repetition.

Supporting this conclusion, in a sense, is an experiment conducted at a recent workshop during which faculty of Ohio Valley College in West Virginia agreed to take the American College Test (ACT) required of entering freshmen. Before the test, attitudes were mixed. "I hope there are plenty of questions on music," said a professor in that department. The English and social science teachers expressed the modest opinion that they would do well on at least one section but warned everyone in advance about how poorly they would do on math and science. The math and science teachers, conscious of their quantitative skills and confident of their literacy, smiled quietly.

The results partly confirmed the expectations. The math and science teachers scored extremely well on the math and quite well otherwise, to lead the faculty overall. The English teachers did the best of anyone on the English test, and the historians did best in their field. Teachers who did not teach core curriculum courses did less well but still outperformed most freshmen. The faculty's average composite was 26, quite respectable for men and women who hadn't studied geometry or balanced a chemical equation in twenty or thirty years.

Despite having become specialists, faculty members still possessed strong basic skills and general knowledge. Many of those young enough to have taken the ACT as high school seniors noted with some surprise and satisfaction that they scored this time about what they had scored in high school. All in all, the test suggested that faculty members had retained more of their high school education than they had expected.

The Risks of Pretests

Whatever it may add to the student's fund of knowledge and competence, the general education offered in colleges builds on a secondary education. If colleges test on material previously learned in high school—whether in English composition, mathematics, or U.S. history—they can never be certain they are testing the value they themselves have added. Even critical thinking and problem-solving skills are already highly developed in many students before they come to college. Assessment of the value added by colleges and universities obviously must involve a reliable pretest, as well as a comprehensive posttest, if it is to have full validity.

College assessment not only runs the risk of measuring high school education but also may err in simply testing the student's individual ability, rather than what the college has taught. Since all Ohio Valley students are required to read through the Bible as part of their general education, they are given a general Bible knowledge test during the first week of classes. For the past two years, the freshman with the highest ACT composite score has also made the highest score on the Bible knowledge test. When they take the test again at the end of the sophomore year, these students are likely to earn the highest grades again. After all, if they initially scored in the 90s while the class average was in the 50s, how much improvement will they have to make to lead the pack as sophomores? Virtually none.

The point is that strong students challenge the process of assessment—even assessment of knowledge in a highly specific domain—because they bring so much knowledge and innate ability and so many generic learning skills with them. Students in selective colleges, for example, may score well on standardized tests that measure general education, not because they have learned so much from their professors but either because they already had a sound general education before college or because they were successful autodidacts during college.

Assessment of general education, of general learning skills, or of basic intellectual tools inevitably aims at the masses rather than at the elite. For that reason, the rationale for using this type of assessment is greater in nonselective colleges (like most private junior colleges) than in elite selective colleges. Even in nonselective colleges, however, good students will skew the results of general assessment.

To summarize briefly, assessing the influence of the first two years of college on a student's general education is no trivial pursuit. Testing details appears to be inadequate because students learn different details and can be expected to remember them only vaguely anyway, if not in the short run at least in the long. Testing for basic or generic skills proves little unless the same test is administered at entrance and again later, because college students bring with them many basic skills from high school. Such testing runs the risk of proving the obvious when good students are involved and, at best, merely indicates a minimal standard of achievement in the context of "higher education."

Complicating all of this is the fact that many students in four-year colleges defer significant parts of their general education until the junior or senior year. Junior colleges stand almost alone in requiring that the general education be completed in four semesters. They are therefore perhaps in the best position to assess the effectiveness of undergraduate general education, separate and apart from the influence of specialized studies.

Testing Cognitive Versus Affective Domains

Testing knowledge and intellectual skills—the cognitive domain—has been the focus of this chapter so far. Many of those involved in supervising the assessment of student development in private colleges, however, find this woefully inadequate. Private colleges are expected to offer a multidimensional learning experience. In order to justify their higher tuition, they feel at least some obligation to prove that their students acquire more content and superior intellectual skills than students at public institutions, that their students show greater personal, affective development, or both propositions. This is a heavy burden, since these colleges often have fewer resources with which to accomplish such objectives than state-supported institutions do.

The affective domain is particularly crucial. If assessment is proving our worth, surely it must measure the worth of a private college education that goes beyond cognitive skills. But how can the private junior college rigorously demonstrate that students develop a commitment to lifelong learning, to humanitarian service, to creative thought, to civic virtue, to moral discrimination, or to Christian sensitivity? Testing for affective development is better conducted with an opinion poll or with personal interviews than with a multiple-choice test. Even so, the effect may be influenced by many factors extraneous to the college. Students may radically change their values, attitudes, and beliefs through church involvement, political action, volunteer work, or association with peers. These changes may or may not have any connection with the college's announced objectives.

Before colleges can confidently hope to measure the affective change they themselves have purposely and systematically caused, they will probably need to define the intended change more precisely. Still, it may be unwise for colleges, even private colleges, to put too much emphasis on affective development. To do so would be, to some degree, to diminish the college's identity as an *academic* institution. Many institutions in society address the affective side of human beings; few concentrate on developing the higher powers of intellect. Outside the college or university, there is little or no emphasis on systematic, rigorous learning for learning's sake. Corporate education is vocational and technical. Few other groups have the resources to provide or insist on a high level of content *and* performance.

In American education, there is already so much emphasis on the extracurricular (to the detriment of the curricular) that undue stress on the affective may only increase the imbalance. Each college must decide whether this imbalance is a consciously willed characteristic of its educational program. Only then should assessment of affective development predominate.

A Workable Approach to Assessment

With all of this in mind, what is a sensible, workable, affordable approach to assessing the value we try to add to students' lives? One inescapable administrative truth is that complicated programs will collapse under their own weight. Any intelligent person can come up with a program; few, however, are able to implement it successfully and keep it going year after year. If a plan isn't simple and convincing, it will never make a permanent transition from theory to practice. No plan can ever be ideal for every college. What follows is a description of the process I followed in formulating a plan of assessment for Ohio Valley College. I began by answering a series of questions prepared by the College-Level Examination Program (1986).

What Are the Aims of Your Specific College? Ohio Valley College is a private junior college that prepares students for transfer to senior colleges. It aims to provide a general education in a Christian context.

What Should Students Learn? They should learn the skills they will need to be successful in advanced studies (for example, oral and written communication, computer literacy, appropriate mathematical skills), and they should obtain the "furniture" of the educated mind (familiarity with history, science, literature, the fine arts, and, in our case, the Bible). They should also show ability in critical thinking and problem solving because the process of learning is often more important than the product and because the proof of any educational experience is in its application to life.

How Can This Be Measured and Who Will Measure It? Basic skills of thinking, speaking, writing, computing, and problem solving should first and foremost be determined by faculty members, who judge on an absolute rather than a relative scale. It is always better to refuse to pass students in the freshman year than to inform them at the end of their sophomore year that they are unprepared for upper-division studies. With a slew of passing grades on their transcripts, students might justifiably ask, "Why aren't we?"

Serving as checks and balances to classroom evaluation could be exit interviews (to measure ability through speaking), writing samples (to test writing and thinking skills), and standardized or locally developed tests (to measure knowledge in mathematics, problem solving, and "furniture"). However, since the faculty again must bear the workload of such an evaluation, the likelihood of long-term, reliable implementation is slim. What faculty members who have three-class loads may embrace as exciting and worthwhile will be viewed as an intolerable imposition by teachers with five-class loads.

As an affordable and workable compromise, why not readminister the ACT to a random sample of sophomores, as suggested in Northeast Missouri State University's book *In Pursuit of Degrees with Integrity* (1984)? By requiring the ACT for matriculating freshmen, we as a college already proclaim our confidence that the test accurately measures preparation for college studies. Our experience confirms time and again that students with higher ACT scores are almost certain to perform better in class than students with lower scores. If we can use these scores for placement, we can also use them for assessment. Higher scores among sophomores would indicate that those students are generally better educated and better prepared for success in upper-division work than they were when they first took the test. Using this method of assessment, the administration bears the workload of assessment, sacrificing some accuracy and comprehensiveness for the sake of the faculty's time, the college's money, and the assessment program's chances of survival.

How Would the Results Be Used? Readministering the ACT would raise the faculty's awareness of its effectiveness and inform students of their progress or lack of progress. If students have been certified by their grade point averages as fit for graduation, poor results on the test should not disqualify them. If such discrepancies are common, the institution must examine itself long before penalizing individual students. Good results, however, should be a feather in the student's cap—something for professors to mention in letters of recommendation.

Admittedly, this is a simple, perhaps even simplistic, plan of assessment; but the cost of a sophisticated plan of assessment is prohibitive for most private junior colleges. It makes sense to use the ACT not only for admissions and placement but also for assessment. The evidence that faculty members do well on it in general, and that faculty members trained in particular subject areas do especially well in those areas, indicates that the test is a valid measure of general education and of competence in the basic areas of English, mathematics, social science, and natural science.

Earlier this year, when a random sample of Ohio Valley College sophomores took the ACT again, three-fourths improved their earlier scores in English, social science, and natural science, while only one-half went up in math. This accurately reflects the reality that while we do require a mathematics course in the core curriculum, the level of proficiency required to satisfy that requirement is not particularly demanding and should perhaps be scrutinized.

The ACT assessment is currently undergoing significant change. It remains to be seen whether colleges will find the new test as useful as the old. Whatever the case, the ACT or one of its rivals needs not be the sole measure of development. It can be supplemented with locally developed tests in domains unique to the college. For example, Ohio Valley uses the general Bible knowledge test not only as a pretest but also as an exit examination. Warren Wilson College in North Carolina is in the process of developing a local test geared to measuring the success of the college's work program, a central part of its educational program.

Still other refinements can be made without too much cost in time and money. Students could be asked to complete questionnaires about campus climate, changes they perceive in themselves since matriculation, and personal commitments. In the days prior to commencement ceremonies, graduates might write "letters" to the college, articulating their ideas about college life—how it benefited them and how it could be improved. A tripartite profile such as this (test scores, questionnaire results, and letters) would fulfill the accrediting agencies' requests for a variety of procedures without overburdening either the financial or human resources of small private colleges.

For colleges that have money to devote to sophisticated assessment, other options are certainly available. One is to hire the faculty of different colleges to conduct interviews as outside evaluators. Educational Testing Service provides a less expensive alternative with a new instrument, the "Academic Profile," which is designed to measure general education. One-hour forms of this multiple-choice test purport to give an institutional profile in the areas of critical thinking, problem solving, reading, writing, and computational skills as they apply to the humanities, natural sciences, and social sciences. A three-hour variation of the test claims to provide accurate individual profiles of achievement. Also available are the ACT COMP tests that aim to differentiate the college level from the high school level in the areas of reasoning and communication skills. A host of other tests have been coming on the market each year.

To learn the most from these tests, of course, colleges must give them to incoming as well as outgoing students. It is not only expensive to do this but also frustrating sometimes. Some freshmen, already confident of admission and placement, are likely not to take these "extra" tests seriously. They may simply go through the motions or not show up at all. Likewise, graduating students may frustrate assessors by giving less than their best on the eve of their long-awaited liberation.

Conclusion

Assessment is an approximate science. Students who don't take classes seriously are also unlikely to take global assessment seriously. Administrators will only frustrate themselves if they expect an expensive, super-sophisticated model of assessment to yield an equally high degree of statistical accuracy. Students don't always cooperate with our best-laid plans. Then again, the multiple-choice test has its limitations, as does any global evaluation given on a particular day to an indifferent group of people. Despite efforts to measure the value we add, the ultimate proof of our effectiveness as colleges lies in the student's long-term success in life after college—and that means success as a person, even more than success as a wage earner.

For schools with adequate funds and personnel, longitudinal studies are appropriate, but they themselves remain only approximations because colleges lose track of some graduates, and many of the less successful ones simply don't respond to questionnaires. It is important, then, to take assessment seriously without taking it too seriously.

Nothing can really replace the semester-by-semester evaluations made by faculty, because teaching and learning are grass-roots activities. Administrators should never become so enamored of their own schemes that they forget where the subtlety of learning is best observed—in the classroom. The aim of assessment is not to improve institutional research; it is to improve teaching and learning by informing the faculty of the curriculum's strengths and weaknesses in attaining its major objective: the intellectual development of students.

Assessment for purposes of institutional research aims at the macrocosm; classroom assessment aims at the microcosm. Just as we measure the universe with less precision than we measure our own planet, it stands to reason that global assessment's role is that of check and balance, rather than definitive judgment. The modern college curriculum has often been condemned for being irrelevant, fragmented, unfocused, and ineffective. But surely there is no reason why the core curricula of most colleges, when handled with integrity, cannot consolidate or confirm a general education appropriate to the maturity of young men and women. The many highly educated graduates of the past are adequate proof.

"If every man would keep his own doorstep clean," said Goethe, "the whole world would be clean." If we preserve the integrity of the curriculum by clarifying our objectives and improving classroom testing procedures, grading policies, and academic standards, grade point averages will become less suspect, and the need for academic data gathering and reporting will become less imperative. At a time when colleges are accused of overcharging and overspending, we must reassure influential men and women of our credibility while still saving every possible dollar for our highest priority: putting good teachers and serious students in an environment conducive to learning.

References

College-Level Examination Program. *Outcomes Assessment in Higher Education: College Administrators' Workshop, Fall 1986*. Princeton, N.J.: College Entrance Examination Board, 1986.

Hirsch, E. D., Jr. *Cultural Literacy: What Every American Needs to Know*. Boston: Houghton Mifflin, 1987.

Northeast Missouri State University. *In Pursuit of Degrees with Integrity: A Value-Added Approach to Undergraduate Assessment*. Washington, D.C.: American Association of State Colleges and Universities, 1984.

John H. Williams is vice-president for instruction at Ohio Valley College, Parkersburg, West Virginia.

Church-related junior colleges that have increased their institutional strength over the years by serving the needs of a more diverse student body are successful not merely by chance.

Expanding the Religious Heterogeneity of the Student Body

George D. Fields, Jr.

This chapter deals with the need and the ability of church-related private junior colleges—which represent the majority of private liberal arts junior colleges—to look outside their own religious affiliation to broaden their base of potential students. The flip side of this theme is the examination of ways to bring more diversity to the college experience. Two perplexing questions push constantly for answers: How much of this is possible in today's cultural and educational climate? Where are the ideas and resources to do it?

An expanded student body based on religious diversity would be helpful to most church-related colleges. Yet the differences between these colleges make it difficult for the administrator of any particular institution to generalize the concept; these differences make it difficult to apply the ideas and approaches of one institution to many others. As one authority describes the problem and the potential, "The commendable pluralism in independent higher education is at the institutional level— the distance from Antioch to Oral Roberts is great, but within each institution, student differences are small. One could easily expand the student diversity within each campus" (Hodgkinson, 1986, p. 12).

Most two-year colleges, including church-related institutions, were founded to provide educational services to new groups. Roueche and Baker (1987, p. 3) suggest that William Rainey Harper expanded the base of higher education in 1898 when he first used the term "junior college" at the University of Chicago and summarized the effect of the movement by saying, "Nearly everyone who has written about the community college alludes to this unique American institution as a democratizing force in higher education."

National statistics on two-year church-related colleges are rather pessimistic and indicate a pressing need for developing potential new-student groups. Only seventy-one church-related colleges remain among the 1,222 regionally accredited community, junior, and technical institutions that operate 1,505 campuses in the United States (Mahoney, 1986). In the last thirty years, our sector has declined from being a substantial partner in the national two-year college system to its present small and shrinking minority status. The Division of Higher Education of the United Methodist Church reports that the number of its two-year colleges declined from seventeen in 1979 to twelve in 1987. Four of these colleges began granting baccalaureate degrees.

This chapter, taking the form of a case study, will briefly describe why and how one specific institution, Spartanburg Methodist College (SMC), in Spartanburg, South Carolina, has changed its religious constituency. SMC has resisted the national trends and grown during the past twenty-five years by strengthening and broadening its religious activities. The college's student body has become far more diverse religiously because of the institution's concerted efforts to expand its enrollment base.

SMC, like most other independent colleges, is enrollment driven, evidenced by the fact that 70 percent of its educational and general budget revenue comes from tuition and fees. In addition to sharing the heavy challenges that every independent college faces, the church-related college has a unique problem in its admissions efforts because its religious mission could limit its appeal to a narrow range of students. Yet, in struggling with this problem, SMC has discovered new resources useful in the very competitive struggle against other institutions for students.

Develop the Church-Related Advantages

The best starting place in any plan for expansion is to understand the intensity of the marketing battles for students. A strong offense is needed; a good defense alone can, at best, bring only a gradually shrinking base of students. One effective means to advance and expand church-related colleges is to broaden the religious constituency of students and the program diversity to meet the needs of new students. Without a well-planned institutional effort, the student constituency is gradually narrowed by the constraints of institutional mission and demographics. Also, competition with state colleges could diminish a church-related college's appeal in today's culture. Only a strong, institutionwide plan, forcefully executed, can minimize the effects of inherent problems created by church relatedness and at the same time capitalize on those opportunities that result from the uniqueness of the institution.

The SMC approach is to make the church relationship very visible and apparent. The name itself signals the religious relationship immediately. A visitor to campus quickly sees religious symbols as predominant features. In 1976, an octagonal-shaped chapel was built in the center of campus to symbolize the hub of a wheel. A towering cross beside the chapel is the most visible architectural feature on campus. The college changed its name in 1974 from Spartanburg Junior College to Spartanburg Methodist College to make its religious nature very apparent.

Chickering (1981) emphasizes the importance of clarity and consistency of objectives and the need to project a clear image of the college's priorities and associations to attract students and meet institutional goals. Over the last twenty years, SMC has changed gradually from a traditional junior college serving 650 full-time students to an institution offering a wide diversity of academic programs and serving 1,030 students.

Most of SMC's students in 1967 were either Methodist or Baptist, and most were white. Of that enrollment, one-third have been lost to state colleges developed in the region. However, new institutional efforts have replaced these lost students with other student types, causing an overall enrollment increase of 58 percent. The present student body comes from diverse racial, cultural, and religious backgrounds. Also, the ages of students now range from seventeen to seventy. In fact, 600 of the present 1,030 students at SMC are served in college programs that did not exist in 1965.

The driving force in expanding the diversity of the student body can be a strong sense of mission to serve people. A college's sense of religious mission to help people can quickly motivate and marshal resources for an expansion of its service capacity to groups of people that are not well served by other institutions. Sister Kathleen Ross, president of Heritage College, describes a better future of independent colleges based on rediscovery of a mission for service:

> The challenge is to remain true to our founding spirit. Virtually all independent institutions came into being to serve a Low Participation Rate [LPR] group. The real problem today is to rekindle that mission. For if we are to assure future socioeconomic stability and growth, to say nothing of justice, independents must provide collegiate education to the new LPR groups [Ross, 1986, pp. 14–16].

A concern for people, coupled with the flexibility of the two-year college, can result in much quicker responses than those of either four-year independent colleges or colleges operating in large governmental systems (Cohen and Brawer, 1982). A strong sense of religious compassion and concern for persons brings new types of students to a church-related college. For instance, five years ago, through the SMC criminal justice classes for corrections officers at a state prison twenty miles from campus, it was discovered that no college opportunities existed for inmates. From this discovery, SMC gained seventy students each year who study in freshman classes provided in the prison.

The start-up phase of the inmate program faced problems that seemed impossible to solve. The lack of an experienced staff and faculty to work with such students and the fact that prisoners have no funds to pay tuition and fees almost terminated the project in the planning stage. In those early days, a trustee, from a proper business perspective, asked at a finance committee meeting, "Why do we have these prison classes when we must raise $55,000 more each year just to keep them going?" Now, after five years, even contributors appreciate the prisoners' personal development through education and the 6 percent of the college's total enrollment the inmates represent, and they count the cost small compared to the value of the program. And it began with a sense of religious mission and concern as well as educational need.

An expanding church-related college directs its academic program toward the various needs of all people in its service area. Strong academic programs with unique religious natures can appeal to a diverse range of persons. In fact, once a two-year college discovers the powerful resources inherent in its church relationship, the odds in the admission struggle are more easily managed. The admission efforts at church colleges do not have to start off at a tremendous disadvantage from state institutions. Church relatedness can be turned into an advantage if new programs are developed quickly to serve the emerging needs in the region and to attract traditional students. Astin (1977) and Bowen (1977) note the power of clearly focused programs offered in an environment that facilitates total student development.

To be successful, the church-related two-year college must master the typical inferiority complex created by comparison with the large and well-financed community college system. The church-related college is not new to higher education, having been in the mainstream for centuries. When the government was still mainly regulating tariffs, passing laws, and fighting wars, churches were creating colleges and educating persons for a life of responsibility and service. The unique value for various types of people is well proved by centuries of academic performance by the educational institutions of many churches. It is important, therefore, to remember the potential that exists today as a result of a long and very strong heritage.

Execute Strong Planning

The church-related college that seeks to expand the number of its students from outside its religious affiliation must develop a sound plan.

This plan should address the institution's essential needs and the problems created by demographics. Spartanburg Methodist College, for instance, has many severe disadvantages in building a heterogeneous student body. The word "Methodist" in the college's name communicates a sectarian institution and could discourage students if not handled properly. Also, while South Carolina supplies 95 percent of the enrolled students, only one of every nine church members in that state is United Methodist—and those few students also have the option of attending three senior United Methodist colleges in the state.

The disadvantage is even more severe in that more than 50 percent of the enrollment is commuting students from the local county, where the United Methodist religious preference is much lower even than in the broader service region. Additionally, in a county of 220,000 people, there are four other institutions of higher education: two four-year independent colleges, one four-year branch of the state university, and a state community college. One of these local colleges, Wofford College, is also affiliated with the United Methodist Church. Even in the midst of this competitive demographic dilemma, however, it is possible to build a successful program.

The plans of the church-related two-year colleges should foster intentional institutional change and development (Bergquist and Armstrong, 1986). Change cannot be instituted quickly enough if it comes only in response to demographic changes. Quick governmental, economic, and cultural changes can leave a college without a student body unless campus leaders are current in their thinking and flexible in their planning. The stronger colleges try to stay ahead of environmental change and position themselves where future students will be. The great potential for expanding the religious heterogeneity of the student body and the diversity of the college experience should be developed into a plan that uses the college's available resources. It is in this approach that colleges weakened by enrollment problems can find new life. Also, strong institutions can become stronger with students from a wider variety of religious backgrounds served in a diverse college experience on campus.

Go for Specific Target Groups

A college working to expand its religious heterogeneity and the diversity of its college experience should develop plans to attract at least three different target groups. These plans should set goals and develop activities to attract students from its own church as well as from other churches and from the general public. The plan to attract each target group should address institutional needs, use available resources, and take into account religious demographics.

Members of the Parent Church. A church-related college is strongest when it maintains a solid core of students from its parent church. Increasing the number of students from a college's own church is not an easy task; many institutions have found it to be a real challenge. For instance, there are 104 United Methodist colleges and universities in the United States that campaign and work hard to attract the students of the parent church. The Division of Higher Education (1987) reports that the mean percentage of United Methodists in student bodies in 1986-87 was 10.7 percent in universities, 21.3 percent in comprehensive colleges, 22 percent in liberal arts colleges, and 28 percent in two-year colleges.

In 1984, SMC began a five-year plan to reverse declining enrollment of Methodist students and increase their percentage among the institution's five hundred resident students from 23 percent to 33 percent and among commuting students from 12 percent to 18 percent. Also, the plan called for decreasing dependency on Baptist students by increasing the numbers from other churches that were underrepresented on campus. In the fourth year of the program, new vitality and strength came with increases in the sought-after students, and the plan is on schedule to reach its goals in the 1989-90 academic year.

The plan to expand religious diversity on campus should require designation of a director to be held accountable for results. At SMC, the campus minister directs the efforts to increase the number of United Methodists and other underrepresented churches. Since this special religious effort is an auxiliary program, the regular admissions staff continues its standard marketing procedures. Activities include a direct mail campaign to parents and students, special data files on names and addresses acquired from churches and processed by the college's computer, and visitations in churches.

Also, a special package of incentives was developed for United Methodist students. Small scholarships are provided to every United Methodist student recommended by the local church minister. Other scholarships are offered to all churches for students with church experience in choirs, drama groups, and local church leadership. Also, need-based financial aid funds have been set aside to cooperate with local churches in helping enroll worthy students who would not otherwise be able to afford the cost of attending SMC.

Students from Other Churches. Most church colleges cannot exist just on students from their own churches. A program similar to that for attracting students from a college's own church also can appeal to students and families in other churches. Baptists, for example, make up 50 percent of SMC students and comprise 57.7 percent of all church members in the region. In the last four years, the dependency on Baptist students has been lessened by increasing the numbers from underrepresented churches. Still, the demographics of the region dictate that SMC would become a much smaller college without its Baptist students.

Long-term success in attracting students from other denominations is maintained through meaningful linkages with those local churches in a college's service area. Various activities help develop these linkages. Student groups, such as choral groups, the Fellowship of Christian Athletes, and drama groups, make favorable impressions when university personnel visit churches. Summer sports camps, in cooperation with various churches, create lasting impressions on children, youth, and the denominational leadership. Colleges that share facilities and staff with local churches create linkages that later bring students to the campus.

At SMC, a new parish of Roman Catholics used the campus chapel as its church for nine years while raising funds to build its own facility. This congregation has brought immense cultural and religious diversity to the campus. Not the least of its contributions to the campus has been the increase in the number of Catholic students in the student body.

Students Without Church Affiliations. A college's mission is to educate, not evangelize. People without church affiliation need the same development and educational preparation as all others for participation in modern life. A church college that implements its public mission without dogmatism serves the nonreligious student well. By supplying a quality education in a meaningful environment, church-related colleges provide an opportunity even for the nonreligious to search for truth. This also applies to the large number of students who list a religious affiliation at registration but who come from homes with little or no active church participation.

The needs for employment, economic security, peace of mind, and healthy relationships are universal. Parnell (1985, p. 98) challenges educators with the potential to educate all people: "One of the great dilemmas for educators is how to meet the great range of individual differences among students while seeking the best in all people, whether rich or poor, able or disabled." Education is a powerful means to help persons, both the religious and nonreligious, meet their life concerns (Bowen, 1977; Parker, 1978). Nonreligious students contribute to campus life by bringing another dimension to the college experience.

The church-related college is strongest when it advocates the place of religious values and the worship of God in the educated person. This appeal hits a responsive chord in the general public, even for many who do not have active church habits but who still seek answers to some of the deeper questions of life. Again, Parnell (1985) helps educators understand this need in all students: "The humanities, the liberal arts, and the fine arts are as important to the electronic technician as they are to the engineer. Caring, compassion, and understanding, the central focus of a liberal education, can help all of us who live and struggle together on this single globe called Earth" (Parnell, 1985, p. 10).

The two-year church-related college should not back away from its relation to the church when recruiting prospective students in fear of losing the nonreligious prospect. The church-related college's unique approach in higher education should be presented clearly to prospective students and parents on visitation days, at orientation sessions, and in admissions material distributed in both publications and media.

Find the Resources

Once a church-related college finds a new potential group that would expand its college experience, it must find the resources of money and people to implement these plans. Sister Kathleen Ross (1986, pp. 14-16) advises independent colleges about the need for new strategies for developing plans and resources required to serve low participation rate (LPR) groups:

> The cornerstone of any action agenda regarding LPR groups must be a recognition that the costs of serving LPR groups in higher education are not those of bricks and mortar. They are the costs of additional scholarships and financial aid for students; developing new student recruitment strategies; hiring appropriate faculty and staff to serve the new population; and long-term faculty development. Perhaps the time has come to change some of our fund-raising priorities . . . specifically to serve LPR groups appropriate to each institution's mission. . . . A change-over to investing in human resources will take coordinated expert planning on the part of our creative development office leadership.

Foundation grants are available to assist colleges in beginning programs to locate and serve persons who are underrepresented and whose lives can be developed by the college's services. During the last year, two national foundations provided program grants for a minority recruiting program at SMC. The college will work mainly through black churches and community groups to interpret the program to both traditional students and working adults.

While these programs usually are not directly related to any particular denominations, many of the activities are handled through churches and bring students representing new religious affiliations to campus. These programs develop cooperative links between the college and an expanded church constituency that produces new students.

Institutions can increase denominational support by requesting funds for particular programs to serve target groups. In an era when denominational support has declined or ceased in many colleges, several have increased their support by requesting funds to serve target groups that have more fund-raising appeal than previous institutional support programs.

Leadership of Trustees, Faculty, and Staff

The breadth and variety of a student constituency, in the long run, will be largely affected by the breadth of the college's leadership in its trustees, faculty, and staff. A marketing blitz and a good admissions plan cannot reverse a narrow institutional perspective created by leadership.

Student heterogeneity is very difficult to generate and then maintain in an institution with a leadership largely confined to one religious belief or to members of a single denomination. Certainly, in order to function well, the leadership of a church-related college needs a sense of religious imperative about life and a concern for people, but narrow denominational requirements fail to create the type of campus community that can expand enrollments from other churches or make a diverse group of students feel a part of the campus community. Trustees, faculty, and staff should bring a breadth of cultural and religious perspectives to a college and be actively involved in many churches and civic organizations. This heterogeneity in leadership is necessary to broaden the college's appeal and meet the needs of students once they have enrolled.

Consultants Help in Planning and Communications

Most church-related colleges need help in interpreting themselves to prospective students. Even the best-trained staff in most small colleges often find it difficult to communicate their real worth and value in ways that are meaningful to students. As a college develops a more diverse student body, the problem of communication and understanding between faculty or staff and students becomes more acute. Again, Ross (1986, pp. 14-16) helps the independent college understand the need for understanding students from different cultures:

> The task is essentially to train faculty and administrators about the consequences of cultural differences. . . . Faculty and those administrators who interact frequently with students need to understand the impact on both students and teachers of subliminal culture (also called primary or covert culture). Subliminal culture is the nonverbalized and often subconscious expectation of appropriate behavior which every culture has.

Prospective students often cross church colleges quickly off their lists. An institution's name, religious symbols, and the student's own perceptions of church and religion hinder many from seeing the real value of a church-related college. Convincing students of the value of specific institutions requires the help of consultants who understand the young-adult culture, the mission of the institution, and effective ways to influence students' decisions.

Many college administrators do not effectively understand the how's and why's of student choice. Bok (1986) and Boyer (1987) describe the diversity, competition, and critical nature of the college selection process and the value of undergraduate education in the lives of students. Consultants can help administrators place a college's real value into thought patterns, images, and sounds that young adults and older youth can digest emotionally and intellectually as they decide on a college. Church-related colleges must interpret their religious missions and the nature of their academic and student service programs in ways perceived positively by prospective students.

In today's culture of persuasive advertising, academic and religious administrators need the help of consultants to shape a convincing message and develop effective media for communicating with a diverse student market. The marketing campaign must be more substantial than simply using glitzy brochures to attract students. The college also must marshal its resources into effective academic and extracurricular programs to meet the expectations of a more diverse student body. Neither marketing nor religion can take the place of a viable and strong academic program, a commitment by the institution to excellence, a strong faculty and staff, and adequate facilities.

A Theology for Expanding Religious Heterogeneity

The theological perspective for expanding the religious diversity of the student body should focus mainly on the central beliefs of the parent church that encourage relationships with students from other church backgrounds as well as the nonreligious. Today's church-related college, which brings diverse persons together for study, inquiry, and celebration of life, needs strength and direction from a sense of theology that helps unite this diversity into a campus community.

Most churches share the major beliefs about the being and nature of God and about the essential aspects of religious life. Usually only a small portion of the parent church's beliefs constricts a college to keep it from serving persons of many other religious backgrounds. Also, many students find it exciting to be in a somewhat different religious environment if their positions are respected and considered seriously. While a strong marketing program is essential for success in today's fierce competition for students, a religious college can easily lose its uniqueness without a theological foundation and understanding of its involvement in the lives of people.

When church-related colleges lose their religious uniqueness, they lose the best reason for asking people to pay typically higher fees to attend. An institution's statement of mission becomes more compelling when it describes how human life can be developed and changed for good and how education provides the process for this change.

A theological foundation for religious diversity on campus helps a college explain its educational purpose to the parent church. This relationship usually carries some tension. A college that moves too far from the parent church can expect repercussions and loss of some friends and funds. Church leaders, and even lay members, tend to want their colleges to uphold and teach the church's particular beliefs, life-styles, and heritage. A college that has a clear theological perspective is able to keep the parent church ties stronger even while serving a majority of students from other churches.

A theological foundation helps the faculty shape the academic requirements in the curriculum. Religious studies required for associate degrees give a theological understanding within a proper academic process and are more positive and motivational than those that come through denominational pressure.

At SMC, a sense of the importance of the Judeo-Christian value system for contemporary life led the faculty to introduce an interdisciplinary course in humanities, in addition to the religion course required for the associate degree. This humanities course includes studies on contemporary social and international issues, ethical and moral dilemmas, and religious perspectives. A variety of activities, such as panels, small-group discussions, convocations, visiting lecturers, and concerts, provide weekly opportunity throughout the academic year for inquiry into values.

A theological foundation helps a religious college communicate its public mission and contributions to the general society. The roots of citizenship and adult responsibility in Western civilization come largely from the Judeo-Christian heritage. The church-related college has a distinct advantage in relating modern living to these deeper roots of today's culture.

Responsible citizens are essential to the future of national and world society. Being bold enough to offer unique opportunities for developing character and integrity will better enable the church-related college to serve a larger and more varied student body.

A theological foundation helps maintain that unique religious concern for the individual person. The church college must be sensitive in its compassion and concern for students, not only for the purpose of satisfying its mission but also as good business practice. Peters and Austin (1985, p. 4) advocate the importance of taking care of customers as a key to success and larger profits. They apply the same principles to schools: "Likewise, in the school, efficient management of the budget is vital; yet a great school is never characterized by the remark, 'It has a good budget.' The superb school is superb only by virtue of its success in developing its unique customer: the student." The church-related college that offers itself most unselfishly to each student becomes the strongest college.

This theological understanding of the value God places on persons leads colleges to develop ways of serving new types of students. In 1984,

SMC began an entirely new type of program in job training for the unemployed. The closing of several textile plants in the region placed thousands of people in unemployment lines. Available jobs required new skills. SMC had teachers and programs to meet their needs but no system to manage the effort. Government funds were available, but the ultimate training goal was a job, not academic credit. The new program required a whole new management system on the campus, but it eventually brought eighty new students and $350,000 in annual revenue.

Conclusion

A church-related college has immense potential to serve a diverse mixture of persons. Such diversity of students creates a more dynamic learning and religious environment. Institutions that have increased their institutional strength over the years by serving the diverse needs of students have been successful not merely by chance. On the contrary, such growth and development result from hard work—in theological inquiry, strong marketing efforts, and academic and institutional development to meet the needs of a diverse student body.

References

Astin, A. W. *Four Critical Years: Effects of College on Beliefs, Attitudes, and Knowledge.* San Francisco: Jossey-Bass, 1977.

Bergquist, W. H., and Armstrong, J. L. *Planning Effectively for Educational Quality: An Outcomes-Based Approach for Colleges Committed to Excellence.* San Francisco: Jossey-Bass, 1986.

Bok, D. *Higher Learning.* Cambridge, Mass.: Harvard University Press, 1986.

Bowen, H. R. *Investment in Learning: The Individual and Social Value of American Higher Education.* San Francisco: Jossey-Bass, 1977.

Boyer, E. L. *College: The Undergraduate Experience in America.* New York: Harper & Row, 1987.

Chickering, A. W., and Associates. *The Modern American College: Responding to the New Realities of Diverse Students and a Changing Society.* San Francisco: Jossey-Bass, 1981.

Cohen, A. M., and Brawer, F. B. *The American Community College.* San Francisco: Jossey-Bass, 1982.

Division of Higher Education. *Comparative Data on United Methodist-Related Colleges and Universities.* Nashville, Tenn.: Board of Higher Education and Ministry, 1987.

Hodgkinson, H. L. *Higher Education: Diversity Is Our Middle Name.* Washington, D.C.: National Institute of Independent Colleges and Universities, 1986.

Mahoney, J. R. (ed.). *Statistical Yearbook of Community, Technical, and Junior Colleges: 1986 Edition.* Washington, D.C.: American Association of Community and Junior Colleges, 1986.

Parker, C. A. (ed.). *Encouraging Development in College Students.* Minneapolis: University of Minnesota, 1978.

Parnell, D. *The Neglected Majority.* Washington, D.C.: Community College Press, 1985.

Peters, T., and Austin, N. *Passion for Excellence: The Leadership Difference.* New York: Random House, 1985.

Ross, K. A. "Making Diversity into a Practical Reality." In H. A. Hodgkinson, *Higher Education: Diversity Is Our Middle Name.* Washington, D.C.: National Institute of Independent Colleges and Universities, 1986.

Roueche, J. E., and Baker, G. A., III. *Access and Excellence: The Open-Door College.* Washington, D.C.: Community College Press, 1987.

George D. Fields, Jr., is president of Spartanburg Methodist College, Spartanburg, South Carolina.

The administration and faculty of two-year colleges must recognize the important contribution that the computer can make now—and in the future—to the education of our students.

Instructional Use of Computers in the Junior College

Gordon L. Wells

Education today faces a tremendous challenge to meet the growing needs of an increasingly technological society. The National Commission on Excellence in Education (1983) points out the mediocrity in our current system and makes dramatic recommendations for reform, including increasing student exposure to computers. Nakhleh (1983) reports on a survey of university computer center directors who predict that by 1990 almost 90 percent of all university students will be computer literate, as will 90 percent of all university faculties and high school students. These predictions, based on current trends, demonstrate the need for educators to incorporate the use of computers into the college classroom.

The purpose of this chapter is to investigate the contribution that computers have made and will continue to make to the educational process in the private liberal arts junior college. Three questions will be addressed:

1. How has the computer been used in the college classroom to date?
2. How effective has this use been?
3. What do the next five years hold for microcomputers in the private liberal arts junior college?

Computer Use in the College Classroom— Current Trends

Many educators feel that the microcomputer offers tremendous potential for the enhancement of the teaching and learning process, and they have compiled lists of potential applications of computers in the classroom. Their lists include the following:

- Keeping attendance and grade books
- Developing personalized student profiles of skills, knowledge, interests, and capabilities to enable the teacher to better motivate and challenge the learner
- Using the technology to stimulate and motivate the learner
- Using computer-assisted instruction (CAI) to drill the learner on facts, tutor the learner on new or difficult materials, provide a self-check on the level of mastery of materials, or allow the learner to simulate laboratory or natural processes
- Helping the learner develop self-confidence.

Ellis (1984, p. 200) cites the ultimate rationale for the use of computers in the classroom as one of necessity: "The rationale for using computers in the classroom is based on our increasing dependence on the creation, use, and communication of information for economic and social well-being. As a result, computing is being recognized as the fourth basic skill."

There have been several attempts to categorize the use of the computer in education. For the sake of simplicity, we will discuss applications of the computer in two-year colleges based on the Taylor model. Taylor (1980) proposes that the computer is used as a tutor, a tool, or a tutee. The "tutor" application is one in which the computer directs the student's learning. Examples are drill and practice, tutorials, games, and simulations. Application programs, such as word processors, data bases, spread sheets, statistical packages, graphics packages, and so on, use the computer in the "tool" mode. A student who programs the computer uses it as a "tutee."

Use of the computer as a "tutor" often comes to mind when computers are mentioned in conjunction with education. Colleges have used traditional CAI for some time now. Instructors use the computer to aid with tutorials, homework problems, examinations, and simulation programs. One of the earliest CAI uses was in drill and practice, little more than electronic programmed texts, or learning machines, that presented a question to a student and then told him or her whether the answer was correct. Over the years, this genre of software has improved with additional discussions of both right and wrong responses, enhanced graphics, and increased branching based on the student's response.

Although some consider this use for drill and practice or tutorials to be a waste of the computer's potential (Thomas, 1983), creative and dynamic programs are being used effectively. Randall (1985) discusses the use of situational questions for a computerized review in biomedical education. Moore (1986) presents two laboratory training programs that use CAI and interactive videocassettes. The addition of the video component, which is managed by the computer, greatly expands the potential of the system for student learning. Computer graphics are now good enough to provide additional enhancement to presentation and review software. Many college students need remedial or supplemental work to help them succeed in their courses. Many private liberal arts junior colleges are unable to afford the additional salaries and other expenses of extra remedial classes. Drill-and-practice programs and tutorials may well meet this need at reduced cost to the institution.

Computer-managed instruction (CMI) systems are designed to administer individualized instructional programs for the student. The computer records and evaluates the student's progress and assigns appropriate instructional activities. The Keller plan of individualized instruction has been modified at the University of Eindhoven, which replaces the tutor with a computer. The computer guides the student's progress and reports to the teacher via printouts. An interesting aspect of this system is that the instructional material is given by the computer, but the testing is done on machine-readable forms (Emck and Ferguson-Hessler, 1980). In contrast, other CMI systems frequently use the computer to administer and grade tests. A related function of the computer is as a diagnostic tool for student evaluation. The student takes an exam or does homework at the computer, and the computer grades the exercise and then provides remedial feedback to the student as necessary. Such testing programs can also provide information concerning the student's problem areas for teacher-directed remediation.

Many educators now feel that one of the most effective uses of the computer in the classroom is in simulation. It is known that different learning tasks require different teaching strategies. Gagné, Wager, and Rojas (1981) suggest that different modes of computerized instruction can be used effectively for different learning needs. For example, drill and practice can effectively provide opportunities for enhancement of skills already learned, while tutorials can provide primary instruction of new material. Gagné, Wager, and Rojas (1981) indicate that simulations help students identify relationships between components of a system and control of the system.

Through simulations, learners have the opportunity to practice with a variety of situations that resemble real-life problems they might face in the future. This type of practice enhances the learner's problem-solving skills.

Simulations provide the learner with an opportunity to apply the scientific method to the solution of problems. Learners are presented with a rich and variable learning environment in which they can master skills and content, develop understanding of concepts, engage in inquiry learning, explore various cause-and-effect relationships, develop strategic thinking, and quickly test multiple hypotheses (Coburn and others, 1982). Further, simulations offer a bridge between concrete and abstract reasoning (Berger, 1984); allow students to postulate abstract concepts in a more concrete manner (Ellis, 1984); convey insight into complicated phenomena and relationships (Goles, 1982); engage student interest and allow the practicing of lab techniques prior to an actual laboratory experience (Nakhleh, 1983); provide the learner with an active role in the learning process (Queen, 1984); provide a realistic cause-and-effect experience in which students can quickly, safely, and efficiently investigate an environment (Shaw, Okey, and Waugh, 1984); help students observe and understand dynamic processes (Switzer and White, 1984); and enhance decision-making skills (Zamora, 1984).

There are many examples of the use of computer simulations in the natural science classroom. Laboratory simulations, such as microcomputer kymographs and electronic burets, allow the student to investigate dangerous or expensive situations safely and cheaply. Tritz (1985) reports the use of a simulation program to investigate bacterial classification based on the IMViC test; he also notes the use of computer simulation in the study of antibiotic sensitivity (Tritz, 1986). Reinecker (1985) describes the use of a computerized clinical simulation in an allied health program, and Randall (1985) discusses the use of physiological simulations. Physics teachers frequently publish articles that present simulations in physics, and chemistry simulations are abundant.

In fact, every discipline appears to have computer simulations available for educational use. The social sciences have used simulations for many years. From historical simulations to simulations on current global conflicts to those modeling world economy, computerized simulations provide increased opportunities for students to investigate their world and develop their thinking skills.

These simulations may prove to be a prime means for educators to tap the power of the computer to help learners develop higher-level cognitive processes and problem-solving skills. According to Shaw, Okey, and Waugh (1984, p. 9), "It is especially in the area of simulations that computers have the potential to deal with higher learning outcomes in a way not previously possible inside the classroom." The computer can keep track of the student's interactions and help the teacher analyze the student's understanding of a problem being investigated in the simulation. The computer serves as problem-solving monitor, coach, and consultant and thus guides the student's learning through discovery.

Taylor (1980) sees the use of the computer as a "tool" as any application that facilitates a given job or task. This is probably the most common use of the computer in the eyes of the general public. Computer software tools include word processors, spread sheets, data-base managers, graphics programs, data-collection and -analysis programs, time management software, and so on. Even teachers at many of the smaller junior colleges use these tools routinely. Computers serve as gradebooks, keep attendance records, generate tests, maintain student profiles, and aid in motivating and challenging students (Goles, 1982; Heard and Tritz, 1982).

Teachers frequently use word processors to generate lecture materials, produce student handouts, communicate with students and their families, and prepare other correspondence. Lesson-planning software allows teachers to generate general plans as well as to prepare individualized plans for students with special needs. The increased availability of multiple fonts has been a tremendous help to the foreign-language teacher. Generating lesson plans, handouts, transparencies, and tests is easier with foreign alphabets and special symbols available in the word processor.

A word processor can also be a valuable tool in the hands of students. Ryan (1986) describes the use of a text processor to teach DNA structure. Other teachers have set up templates for their students to use for typing their reports, required students to turn in papers on computer diskettes, and taught writing on the word processor. The instructor suggests improvements and has the student revise his or her work. Many software packages are available to help the student writer. Idea organizers help—and sometimes direct—the student to construct better paragraphs and sentences. Grammar checkers help improve grammar, and other software helps the writer to construct better topical sentences. Neither the teacher nor the student has to dread the revision process necessary to produce a polished written product.

The computer has often been used as a computational tool. Bowker and Bowker (1986) suggest that the use of the computer to perform repetitive calculations for students improves teaching efficiency in general ecology by freeing time otherwise spent doing calculation for more meaningful and productive teacher/student interaction. Thompson and Bernard (1985-86, p. 210) have students use the computer to rapidly perform statistical analyses on data so that "more time can be spent on meaning rather than computational methods." Programs enable students to enter their data and receive printouts of calculations for accounting, economics, mathematics, psychology, and the natural sciences.

Many teachers use electronic spread sheets (electronic ledgers) to keep their budgets, serve as gradebooks, and perform other administrative functions. These spread sheets can also serve as a functional and versatile tool for students. With strong mathematical capabilities, such software is an ideal tool for students to use for data analysis. Most people familiar with electronic spread sheets recognize their value to the business student. Henderson, however, provides his students with templates into which they enter data files from their experiments. The computer then takes the drudgery out of the calculations and graphing of chemical kinetics data (J. Henderson, personal communication, 1987). Henderson confirms that students in the sciences can also make practical use of this powerful tool. The spread sheet can be programmed to calculate statistics or to perform advanced calculus computations, such as regression analysis (Hsiao, 1985). Wells and Berger (1985-86) demonstrate how teachers and students can use the spread sheet to generate simulations.

Another genre of tool software is computer-generated graphics. Some educators advocate the use of interactive graphics programs to enhance student learning. The implementation of this application has some problems, however, as illustrated by Hepner and Hodler (1982), who point out that students' limited knowledge of computer graphics capabilities and/or lack of understanding of the use of graphics in the analysis process must be addressed if the computer graphics tools are to be used effectively. Brillhart and Bell (1983) describe the effective use of computer-generated graphics as part of students' BASIC programs. They contend that this application of graphics enhances students' understanding of descriptive geometry and computerized drafting and is a powerful tool in developing logical thinking skills.

Microcomputer-based labs (MBLs) use the computer as both a data-collection instrument and a data-analysis tool. As Tinker (1981, p. 94) points out, "The computer-as-instrument can replace more expensive instrumentation in many traditional labs, and make possible some entirely new student experiences." In describing a simple cooling curve experiment, he points out that students could collect data by arming themselves with mercury thermometers and stopwatches, but that automating the collection and plotting of such data is an appropriate use of the microcomputer.

Since the early attempts at interfacing the computer to lab input devices, many articles have been written and workshops presented on the use of the computer in data capture and analysis. These presentations cite the advantages and disadvantages of MBLs and present basic experiments that teachers can use with their students with inexpensive interface devices. Many available commercial interface kits now enable teacher and students to simply plug the devices into the computer, run the software, and select the experiment to be performed from a menu.

Data-base application programs are also a valuable tool for the educator. Teachers use them as gradebooks, to maintain inventories, and to store bibliographies. They are also a powerful instructional tool in the classroom. Students can use them as resources, to investigate concepts of classification, to perform data manipulation and analysis, or to engage in problem-solving activities (Blom, 1984; Suder, 1984).

Many additional "tools" are also available to educators and their students. Puzzle makers, molecular model generators, data bases of pictures, music-writing programs, accounting software, authoring tools, and map generators are just a few of the types of software that have helped educators better communicate with their students. Career guidance and planning software can also be used effectively at junior colleges, which often lack separate career counseling services.

Effectiveness Under Scrutiny

Switzer and White (1984) discuss the place of the computer in the social science classroom. They point out that for the computer, as for any technology, the ultimate objective in the classroom is to enhance learning. They laud the computer's ability to provide an opportunity for learners to develop skills in identifying problems and in seeking, organizing, analyzing, evaluating, and communicating information. They encourage the use of computerized data bases, statistical packages, word processors, spread sheets, and graphics programs to provide these opportunities.

Yet with all of the potential uses, the computer has not found its place in the curriculum of most schools. Many teachers still do not use the computer for instruction, and many more use it only in applications that fail to fully tap its power. It is believed that many computer applications in use in the classroom today help learners develop lower-level cognitive processes but do little for the higher-level processes. Thomas (1983, p. 10) points out that "using a computer solely for drill and practice is akin to buying a programmable calculator to use as a paperweight; you are not realizing the full potential of the tool."

How effective are computers in classroom instruction? Hollen, Bunderson, and Dunham (1971) compare the effectiveness of CAI simulation of a qualitative analysis lab to that of traditional labs and show no significant difference between the groups as to cognitive achievement. They conclude that either CAI or traditional labs can be used to teach the principles of qualitative analysis but that CAI could not develop the manipulative skills. The CAI labs, however, required less student time and made lower demands on facilities and personnel. Ellinger and Frankland (1976) compared computer-assisted instruction to lecture instruction and demonstrated that both methods were equally effective in teaching comprehension and application and equally poor in teaching recall of definitions. They concluded that until the cost of computers dropped, CAI would not be cost-effective, but that the secondary benefits of CAI would make it cost-effective in the future. In the thirteen years since their report, the price of computers has dropped to a point that makes CAI much more cost-effective.

Brown and McMahon (1979) evaluated a computer-assisted management of learning (COMOL) package in a beginning college physics course. They found that able students learning independently improved their grades by using their time more efficiently. Students with less maturity had difficulty coping with self-motivated learning situations and did not progress as well. Cokewood (1980) compared the effectiveness of CAI and programmed instruction to traditional instruction for improving problem-solving skills. He reports no significant difference between the treatments in favor of the CAI.

In an attempt to better quantify the results of years of research on the effectiveness of CAI, meta-analytic techniques are applied (Kulik and Bangert-Drowns, 1983; Kulik and Kulik, 1985). These studies indicate that CAI is an effective tool at the college level, with an effect size ranging from 0.26 to 0.5 (an effect size of 0.5 is equivalent to raising scores from the 50th percentile to the 70th percentile). Additional benefits include small but positive changes in student attitudes toward instruction and computers and substantially reduced instructional time.

Because of the tremendous variety of studies performed and their often conflicting results, investigators have attempted to review the experimental studies and derive some quantitative summary of their results. Okey (1985) investigated the effectiveness of computer-based education (CBE) by compiling reviews of research reports published over a fourteen-year period. He found that, for the most part, CBE is at least as effective as traditional instruction and enhances learning when used in conjunction with traditional instruction. The reviews indicate that subject matter, age of students, type of CBE materials, and objectives being measured all influenced the results of the study. Okey (1985, p. 6) concludes, "No reasonable arguments can be made for failing to use CBE as a supplement to regular instruction in science classrooms. The effectiveness of CBE has been extensively documented over more than twenty years."

Although it appears that CAI can be an effective educational tool, more research is needed on the effectiveness of additional applications of the computer to instruction. Grabe (1984) states that an adequate empirical data base is not available to enable one to argue the benefits or inadequacies of educational computing. Salomon (1984) and Waugh (1985) indicate that more modes of CAI (other than drill and practice and tutorials) need to be evaluated and that more research is needed in subject areas outside of mathematics. He recommends that studies be conducted in nine areas, including computer-assisted laboratory exercises, simulations, testing, interactive videodisc, data-base access, and others.

Academic Potential of the Computer in the Two-Year College

Computer facilities in two-year colleges are significantly different from those at major universities. Not only is the size and quality of facilities different, but the purposes are vastly different. Two-year colleges devote

94 percent of their academic computing time to instruction, while universities devote only 59 percent to instruction (Warlick, 1986). The question to raise at this point is how this 94 percent will be used in the coming years.

One of the issues that will be addressed is computer literacy. Currently there is not a consensus as to what computer literacy is. On one side of the issue is the emphasis on computer awareness and computer programming, and on the other is the emphasis on computer awareness and application. While someone must program computers, it is not essential that every college student be able to program. It is essential, however, that all students be familiar enough with the use of the computer to let it work for them in their schooling as well as in their lives following their school years. The two-year college will, in many instances, be responsible for providing that literacy. Currently, many institutions are providing computer literacy classes for their students, but in the future, literacy will be provided through integration of the computer throughout the curriculum.

This integration will be a major advance during the next several years (Garson, 1987; O'Brien, 1985; Wholeben, 1985). Students will use word processors to produce papers for all of their classes after learning how to write with them in English composition. CAI applications in several classes will help students become comfortable using the machines as they learn their course material, and the use of data bases will allow them to tap resources previously unavailable to them.

In the sciences, students will use the computer more and more for data collection and analysis. Students will set up an experiment, let the computer collect and digest the data, and then spend their time analyzing and synthesizing the results, to better understand the theories and processes involved. They will then exchange their data with other students around the world via electronic networks and telecommunications (Levin and Cohen, 1985; C. Wolfe, personal communication, 1987).

Students in two-year colleges will depend more on telecommunications to access materials unavailable locally. On-line data bases will provide smaller colleges with the equivalent of the library facilities of major universities. Electronic bulletin boards will allow students and faculty to communicate with experts in various disciplines who are currently unavailable to them.

Interactive video will assume a more important place in computerized instruction in the years to come. Videodisc technology will provide a wealth of high-quality graphics for computerized instruction. With the integration of animation, computer simulations will be even more powerful educational tools. The potential has prompted statements like this one: "The videodisc will probably have the greatest effect on the nature of future simulation use in science education" (Marks, 1982, p. 20).

A task force, established at the National Videodisc Symposium held at the University of Nebraska, Lincoln, in November 1986, expressed concern that educators not let the technology fail because of inadequate planning. They advocated that evaluation and research be linked to planning, to ensure that videodisc technology would reach all students (Sybouts, 1987). Lehman (1986, p. 28) views interactive video as a powerful tool for teaching, but he acknowledges that "the final arbiters of the success or failure of interactive video will be the classroom teachers who must accept it, learn to use it, and decide how best to employ this new technology for the betterment of teaching and learning."

The need for individualized instruction to meet the learning needs of each student is often cited in the literature, yet individualized instruction via the computer has not become as widespread as many would like it to be. One of the reasons is that software has been unable to truly evaluate the student's competencies and guide his or her learning in a unique direction tailored to specific needs. A second problem has been the inability of tutorial software to really present and evaluate situations that challenge the student beyond the lower cognitive levels. Many view the development of artificial intelligence and its incorporation into CAI as a potential solution to these weaknesses. Hajovy and Christensen (1987) predict that the next generation of CAI will be characterized in the following ways:

- It will be grounded in learning and instructional theory and will use a comprehensive metalearning model that will truly assess and diagnose the student's learning style.
- It will direct the student's learning accordingly, by choosing the appropriate instructional strategy based on the learning objectives and the material to be learned.
- It will employ informal and formal heuristics from artificial intelligence, to give the program the capacity to learn and adjust to new situations.

Conclusion

In the past fifteen years, spending by colleges and universities on computer technology has risen from $500 million to $1.3 billion annually. The emphasis on computers and computing at the college level has involved more than $70 million in grants from the National Science Foundation and millions more from other sources, such as Title III grants. Soon every college student will be expected to have access to a full range of computing and information services, and this access will be as necessary as access to the library is now (Zucker, 1984).

The administration and faculty of two-year colleges must recognize the important contribution that the computer can make, now and in the future, to the education of our students. Potential reduction in the cost of remediation through the use of advanced CAI programs, use of computer simulation to instruct and encourage critical thinking, improvement in student counseling with career guidance and planning software—these are some of the benefits available with this technology.

As computer capabilities increase and prices drop, two-year junior colleges will find it easier to provide their students access to computers and the services they provide.

If we fail to computerize, we will fail to provide our students with a vital tool in a highly competitive marketplace. Wholeben (1985, p. 94), in an article on the place of computers in higher education, indicates that if we recognize and accept the ingredients for effective data processing, "the computer will prove to be the most significant innovation for use by higher education since Gutenberg's . . . introduction of the printing press."

References

Berger, C. "Learning More Than Facts: Microcomputer Simulations in the Science Classroom." In D. Peterson (ed.), *The Intelligent Schoolhouse: Readings on Computers and Learning*. Reston, Va.: Reston, 1984.

Blom, K. G. "The Microcomputer as a Tool for Teaching Classification." *American Biology Teacher*, 1984, *46* (4), 232-233.

Bowker, L. S., and Bowker, R. C. "Using Computers to Increase Course Efficiency: An Example in a General Ecology Laboratory." *Collegiate Microcomputers*, 1986, *4* (1), 1-6.

Brillhart, L. V., and Bell, E. "Computer Graphics by Students for Students: Enhancing Science Education." *Journal of College Science Teaching*, 1983, *13* (1), 28-31.

Brown, M., and McMahon, H. "Computer-Managed Independent Learning in A-Level Physics." *Physics Education*, 1979, *14* (1), 14-19.

Coburn, P., and others. *Practical Guide to Computers in Education*. Reading, Mass.: Addison-Wesley, 1982.

Cokewood, D. "A Comparison of the Effectiveness of Computer Assisted Instruction and Programmed Instruction in Improving Problem-Solving in College Level Electronics." *Dissertation Abstracts International*, 1980, *41* (4), 1445-A.

Ellinger, R. S., and Frankland, P. "Computer Assisted and Lecture Instruction: A Comparative Experiment." *Journal of Geography*, 1976, *75* (1), 109-120.

Ellis, J. D. "A Rationale for Using Computers in Science Education." *American Biology Teacher*, 1984, *46* (4), 200-206.

Emck, J. H., and Ferguson-Hessler, M.G.M. "A Computer-Managed Keller Plan." *Physics Education*, 1980, *16* (1), 46-49.

Gagné, R. M., Wager, W., and Rojas, A. "Planning and Authoring Computer-Assisted Instruction Lessons." *Educational Technology*, 1981, *21* (9), 17-26.

Garson, G. D. *Academic Microcomputing: A Resource Guide*. Newbury Park, Calif.: Sage, 1987.

Goles, G. G. "Simulation Games: Some Educational Uses and Reviews." *Journal of Computers in Mathematics and Science Teaching*, 1982, *2* (1), 22-24.

Grabe, M. "Evaluating the Educational Value of Microcomputers." *Computers in the Schools*, 1984, *1* (4), 35-44.

Hajovy, H., and Christensen, D. L. "Intelligent Computer-Assisted Instruction: The Next Generation." *Educational Technology,* 1987, *27* (5), 9-14.

Heard, J. T., Jr., and Tritz, G. J. "Training the Medical Student in Computer Usage." *Journal of Computers in Mathematics and Science Teaching,* 1982, *1* (3), 17-21.

Hepner, G. F., and Hodler, T. W. "The Role of Interactive Computer Mapping in the Science Curriculum." *Journal of College Science Teaching,* 1982, *11* (6), 367-368.

Hollen, T. T., Jr., Bunderson, C. V., and Dunham, J. L. "Computer-Based Simulation of Laboratory Problems in Qualitative Chemical Analysis." *Science Education,* 1971, *55* (2), 131-136.

Hsiao, M. W. "Teaching Regression Analysis with Spreadsheets." *Journal of Computers in Mathematics and Science Teaching,* 1985, *4* (4), 21-26.

Kulik, C. C., and Kulik, J. A. "Effectiveness of Computer-Based Education in Colleges." Paper presented at the annual meeting of the American Educational Research Association, Chicago, March 31-April 4, 1985. (ED 263 890)

Kulik, J. A., and Bangert-Drowns, R. L. "Effectiveness of Technology in Precollege Mathematics and Science Teaching." *Journal of Educational Technology Systems,* 1983, *12* (2), 137-157.

Lehman, J. D. "Interactive Video—A Powerful New Tool for Science Teaching." *Journal of Computers in Mathematics and Science Teaching,* 1986, *5* (3), 24-29.

Levin, J. A., and Cohen, M. "The World as an International Science Laboratory: Electronic Networks for Science Instruction and Problem Solving." *Journal of Computers in Mathematics and Science Teaching,* 1985, *4* (4), 33-35.

Marks, G. H. "Computer Simulations in Science Teaching: An Introduction." *Journal of Computers in Mathematics and Science Teaching,* 1982, *1* (4), 18-20.

Moore, J. F. "Laboratory Equipment Training Utilizing CAL and Interactive Videocassettes." *Computer Education,* 1986, *10* (1), 25-28.

Nakhleh, M. B. "An Overview of Microcomputers in the Secondary Curriculum." *Journal of Computers in Mathematics and Science Teaching,* 1983, *3* (1), 13-21.

National Commission on Excellence in Education. *A Nation at Risk: The Imperative for Educational Reform.* Washington, D.C.: National Commission on Excellence in Education, 1983.

O'Brien, T. C. "Computers and Education." *Computer Center,* 1985, *47* (5), 315-316.

Okey, J. A. "The Effectiveness of Computer-Based Education: A Review." Paper presented at the annual meeting of the National Association for Research in Science Teaching, French Lick, Ind., April 1985.

Queen, J. A. "Simulations in the Classroom." *Improving College and University Teaching,* 1984, *32* (3), 144-145.

Randall, J. E. "Microcomputers and Biomedical Education." *American Biology Teacher,* 1985, *47* (3), 176-178.

Reinecker, L. "Computerized Clinical Simulations." *Computer Education,* 1985, *9* (1), 57-66.

Ryan, P. "Using the Text Processor to Teach DNA Structure." *American Biology Teacher,* 1986, *48* (1), 47-48.

Salomon, G. "Computers in Education: Setting a Research Agenda." *Educational Technology,* 1984, *24* (10), 7-11.

Shaw, E. L., Okey, J. R., and Waugh, M. L. "A Lesson Plan for Incorporating Microcomputer Simulations into the Classroom." *Journal of Computers in Mathematics and Science Teaching,* 1984, *3* (4), 9-11.

Suder, R. "Use of the Computer for Chemistry Instruction." *Journal of Chemical Education,* 1984, *61* (3), 243-245.

Switzer, T. J., and White, C. S. "National Council for the Social Studies Position Statement: Computers in Social Studies." Unpublished manuscript, National Council for the Social Studies, 1984.

Sybouts, W. "Videodisc Technology: A National Plan for Its Use in Education." *T.H.E. Journal*, April 1987, pp. 47-48.

Taylor, R. P. (ed.). *The Computer in the School: Tutor, Tool, Tutee.* New York: Teachers College Press, 1980.

Thomas, W. E. "Science-Based Simulation Development: An Example in Physics." *Journal of Computers in Mathematics and Science Teaching*, 1983, *2* (3), 10-16.

Thompson, S. R., and Bernard, F. A. "Accuracy and Precision in Measurement." *Journal of College Science Teaching*, 1985-86, *15* (3), 209-211.

Tinker, R. F. "Microcomputers in the Teaching Lab." *Physics Teacher*, 1981, *19* (2), 94-105.

Tritz, G. J. "Computer Modeling Microbiological Experiments in the Teaching Laboratory: The IMViC Reactions as a Prototype." *Journal of Computers in Mathematics and Science Teaching*, 1985, *4* (4), 41-46.

Tritz, G. J. "An Antibiotic Resource Program for Students of the Health Professions." *Journal of Computers in Mathematics and Science Teaching*, 1986, *5* (3), 51-55.

Warlick, C. H. "Academic Computing Facilities and Services in Higher Education—A Survey." *EDUCOM Bulletin*, 1986, *21* (3), 2-7.

Waugh, M. L. "Proposed Directions for Research in Computer-Based Education." Paper presented at the annual meeting of the National Association of Research in Science Teaching, French Lick, Ind., April 1985.

Wells, G. L., and Berger, C. F. "Teacher/Student-Developed Spreadsheet Simulations: A Population Growth Example." *Journal of Computers in Mathematics and Science Teaching*, 1985-86, *5* (2), 34-40.

Wholeben, B. E. "The Impact of Computerized Technology on the Applied Sciences: A New Direction for Higher Education in the Twentieth Century." *Collegiate Microcomputer*, 1985, *3* (1), 85-95.

Zamora, R. M. "The Pedagogy of Games." In D. Peterson (ed.), *The Intelligent Schoolhouse: Readings on Computers and Learning.* Reston, Va.: Reston, 1984.

Zucker, A. A. "Computers in Education in the U.S.A." In D. Peterson (ed.), *The Intelligent Schoolhouse: Readings on Computers and Learning.* Reston, Va.: Reston, 1984.

Gordon L. Wells is assistant professor and chair of the Division of Natural and Applied Science, Ohio Valley College, Parkersburg, West Virginia.

Are part-time faculty vital, experienced professionals who add to the quality of the private junior college experience, or are they hired to ease the salary burden on the budget? The answer is elusive.

The Adjunct/Full-Time Faculty Ratio

Milton L. Smith

The use of part-time faculty in higher education is neither a new nor a recent practice. In the nineteenth century, colleges and universities frequently used part-time faculty as visiting professors. These visiting professors brought to the students a new perspective on a specific segment of the curriculum. They were also used as experts to fill gaps in the knowledge base of the regular, full-time faculty resulting from the rapid proliferation of scholarly areas of study. Today, part-time faculty are an even more significant segment of the total faculty, constituting 37 percent of the faculty in all of higher education (Snyder, 1987).

Two-Year Colleges

Two-year colleges have been especially involved in the use of part-time faculty because of the colleges' commitment to meeting the needs of the community. Often, two-year colleges offer courses that interest only a small segment of students, or they offer special programs that require the knowledge and skills of current practitioners. In either case, the part-time faculty member is the obvious answer to the situation. Such teachers, working full-time and teaching part-time, keep the colleges' offerings more current and pragmatic. Today, the majority of two-year colleges in the nation use part-time faculty; 56 percent of the total faculty in the nation's two-year colleges are part-time (American Association of Community and Junior Colleges, 1986).

Private Junior Colleges

The private, church-related junior colleges of the mid nineteenth century began the now-recognized major movement in higher education called the community junior college movement. For almost a century, the private junior college played the major role in expanding the junior college movement. Not until the 1947-48 academic year did the number of public junior colleges exceed the number of private junior colleges in the nation. Since that time, the number of private junior colleges has steadily declined. By the end of the 1970s there were six public junior colleges for every private one.

The *1986 Community, Technical, and Junior College Directory*, published by the American Association of Community and Junior Colleges, lists 1,059 public and 141 private junior colleges in the United States, which is a ratio of 7.5 public to each private junior college. (Since 1986, the number of private junior colleges has continued to drop.) However, more than 100,000 students enroll at and more than 7,000 faculty work at those private junior colleges, and institutions in the two-year college movement continue to be significant for research.

The study of the use of part-time faculty in higher education has resulted in a large body of literature. Even when two-year colleges are isolated as a separate category of institutions of higher education, the quantity of literature resulting from the study of part-time faculty is still significant. However, in regard to private junior colleges specifically, it is difficult to find research results. This chapter attempts to pull together and comment on available data concerning the use of part-time faculty in the private junior colleges of the nation.

All references made to current studies and to data, unless otherwise documented, are from two studies that I conducted (Smith, 1981, 1986). In those studies, private junior colleges are categorized as church-related junior colleges; independent, nonprofit junior colleges; and independent, for-profit junior colleges. Data in this chapter are often reported for each of these three kinds of private junior colleges.

The Numbers. An analysis of the use of part-time faculty in private junior colleges reveals that considerable change in the percentage of part-time faculty has occurred from the time that such records have been available. Table 1 presents these changes based on data from 1969 and 1986, a span of seventeen years.

Note that the ratios of full-time to part-time faculty decreased in each category, most notably in the nonprofit sector, where the ratio dropped from 2.1 full-time for every part-time faculty member to 0.9 for 1, a 57 percent reduction. Church-related private junior colleges experienced a 26 percent ratio reduction. The overall result is that in less than two decades the ratio of full-time to part-time faculty for all private junior colleges leveled off at one to one from more than two to one.

Table 1. Full-Time Versus Part-Time Faculty
(Numbers represent those colleges submitting complete data.)

Type	1969 Number of Institutions	Full-Time	Part-Time	FT/PT Ratio	1986 Number of Institutions	Full-Time	Part-Time	FT/PT Ratio
Church-Related	138	2,637	1,144	2.3:1	55	1,455	838	1.7:1
Nonprofit	105	3,584	1,741	2.1:1	48	1,546	1,730	0.9:1
Profit	0	0	0	—	9	327	686	0.5:1
Total	243	6,221	2,885	2.2:1	112	3,328	3,254	1.0:1

Source: 1969 data from the *Junior College Directory*, 1969; 1986 data from the *Community, Technical, and Junior College Directory*, 1986.

The Future. Perhaps the best way to assess the future of part-time faculty in the private junior college is to extrapolate from recent, known data. Table 2 shows the total data from all private junior colleges (including incomplete data from some colleges) as reported in American Association of Community and Junior Colleges directories from 1976 through 1986. Five of the eleven years are reported as having more part-time faculty than full-time faculty employed. Of significance, however, is the fact that four of those five years are the four most recent years. These data seem to indicate that not only will part-time faculty continue to be used in private junior colleges, but they may be in the majority.

Substantiating this prediction are the results of my 1986 study, which showed that 99 percent of the eighty-five private junior colleges included in the study employed part-time faculty. The highest percentage of part-time faculty among those colleges was 96, the lowest was 3, and the average was 50. When asked whether their current number of part-time faculty had increased, decreased, or stayed the same as in the previous year, 35 percent of the respondents indicated an increase.

Expectations

Teaching Load. Part-time faculty in private junior colleges teach widely varying numbers of courses, ranging from one to four per semester or quarter, with an average of 1.6. Most church-related private junior colleges reported an average teaching load of one course, while most independent, nonprofit junior colleges reported two courses as an average load for part-time faculty.

Student Advisement. Many full-time faculty accuse part-time faculty of not assuming their responsibility to the students because they are not available for student consultation and advisement. Full-time faculty often complain that they are left with the total responsibility for those services.

The latest study of this topic in 1986 shows that of the 84 private junior colleges included in the study, 62 percent required no time on campus, other than class time, for part-time faculty to consult with or advise students. Among the 32 institutions that did require student advisement hours, the number of hours varied widely from "unspecified," to five hours per week.

A larger percentage of independent, for-profit colleges (50 percent) required student advisement by part-time faculty than did either independent, nonprofit colleges (33 percent) or church-related colleges (40 percent).

Indicating some improvement in this area, an earlier study in 1981 showed that 73 percent of eighty-four institutions reported no required hours for student advisement. An increase of 11 percent of the colleges in a five-year period shows some concern for the problem and some movement toward its solution.

Table 2. Faculty in Private Junior Colleges: 1976-1986

Year	Full-Time	Part-Time	% Part-Time	FT/PT Ratio
1976	4,076	3,874	49%	1.05/1.00
1977	4,129	4,038	49%	1.02/1.00
1978	4,059	3,611	47%	1.12/1.00
1979	4,013	3,554	47%	1.13/1.00
1980	3,639	3,422	48%	1.06/1.00
1981	3,805	3,887	51%	0.97/1.00
1982	3,841	3,672	49%	1.05/1.00
1983	3,588	3,679	51%	0.97/1.00
1984	3,545	3,708	51%	0.96/1.00
1985	3,733	4,023	52%	0.93/1.00
1986	3,443	3,488	50%	0.99/1.00

Source: Extracted from American Association of Community and Junior Colleges, 1976-1986.

Attendance at Faculty Meetings and Orientation. More colleges require part-time faculty to attend orientation or in-service programs than to attend faculty meetings. The 1986 study shows that only 14 percent required attendance at faculty meetings, while 39 percent required attendance at orientation or in-service programs. One college actually prohibited part-time faculty from attending faculty meetings.

A much larger percentage of independent, for-profit colleges (66 percent) required part-time faculty to attend faculty meetings than did church-related colleges (16 percent) or independent, nonprofit colleges (3 percent). The same figures hold for orientation or in-service programs.

A comparison of the findings of the 1981 and 1986 studies shows only a slight increase in the percentage of colleges requiring attendance at faculty meetings: 13 percent versus 14 percent. The same is true of required attendance at orientation or in-service programs. Although slight, the trend seems to be in a positive direction.

Committee Service. Service on faculty committees is not expected of most part-time faculty, and the trend, as indicated by the 1981 and 1986 studies, is toward even less service. In 1981, committee service was required by 12 percent of the eighty-three institutions in the study; in 1986, only 1 percent required such service. The earlier study shows 3 percent of institutions prohibiting such service; by the later study, prohibition had increased to 5 percent.

These data point up two important facts. First, they lend support to the position of some full-time faculty that they have to carry the noninstructional load of part-time faculty. Second, they show how part-time faculty are made to feel even more removed from the institution. The result could be a reduction in commitment to the goals of the college.

Willingness to remove committee service from the job requirements of part-time faculty was evidenced by a greater proportion of church-related institutions (58 percent) than by independent, nonprofit colleges (45 percent) or independent, for-profit colleges (20 percent). The same order holds for prohibiting committee service: 7, 3, and 0 percent, respectively.

Evaluation. Most part-time faculty in private junior colleges are evaluated on the same basis as are full-time faculty. In the 1986 study, more than eight of ten indicated that there were no differences in the evaluation processes used for full-time and part-time faculty. In some instances, there was no formal evaluation at all for part-time faculty. Fifteen institutions indicated the following differences in the evaluation process:

- Providing for a less formal evaluation for part-time faculty
- Substituting work experience for formal education in the evaluation process
- Eliminating student advisement, committee work, and other service as evaluation criteria
- Substituting a personal interview with an administrator for the evaluation process.

Little difference is noted between the findings of the 1981 and 1986 studies.

If, indeed, more than eight of ten colleges hold both full-time and part-time faculty to the same evaluation criteria, it would seem difficult for part-time faculty to have an equal chance of success unless, of course, the criteria are those related solely to classroom performance and results.

Characteristics

Formal Education. Generalizations are frequently heard about part-time faculty with regard to their formal education. Some critics contend that part-time faculty are less educated formally than those devoting full time to college teaching. Others contend that many part-time faculty are full-time practitioners in their fields and are therefore better prepared in terms of formal education. The 1986 study revealed that 86 percent of the institutions considered part-time faculty equal to full-time faculty in terms of amounts of formal education, with 8 percent showing part-time faculty as less formally educated and 6 percent as more highly educated. The most significant contributors to these results were independent, for-profit colleges, which indicated that nearly one-fourth of their part-time faculty were less formally educated than their full-time faculty.

Teaching Experience. A concern often expressed about the use of part-time faculty is that they might lack teaching experience. They are frequently charged with knowing the content but not knowing how to teach it. While a slight majority of the institutions in the 1986 study reported equal experience between the two groups, 44 percent reported less experience among part-time faculty.

A comparison of these data with data from the 1981 study shows an increase of 10 percent in colleges reporting less teaching experience among part-time faculty and a decrease of 7 percent in colleges reporting equal teaching experience between the two groups. This seems to be a negative trend if teaching experience is considered a significant factor in the selection of faculty.

Sources. Part-time faculty in private junior colleges come from a variety of sources; however, the primary source, as reflected in both the 1981 and 1986 studies, is local business and industry. Forty-one percent of the colleges listed that as first from a list of possible sources. The ranked list from the studies includes the following:

1. Local business and industry employees
2. Qualified community members not otherwise employed
3. High school faculty
4. Faculty from four-year colleges or universities
5. Spouses of faculty members
6. Faculty from other two-year colleges.

While there were no significant differences in the rankings between the two studies, 1986 data show a larger percentage of colleges using local business and industry employees, reflecting the recent trend toward more cooperative efforts between junior colleges and community businesses and industries.

Subject Areas. Part-time faculty are employed to teach a variety of subject areas. The discipline reported most frequently in the 1986 study was business. The ranked list of disciplines, similar in both studies and across types of institutions, includes business, humanities, mathematics, English, science, music, social sciences, and technical skills. The only trend noted between the two studies was an increase in the frequency of employing part-time faculty to teach business-related courses.

Additional Employment. To determine to what extent part-time faculty in private junior colleges hold other employed positions, the institutions in the two studies were asked whether the majority of their part-time faculty were (1) employed full-time elsewhere, (2) employed part-time elsewhere, or (3) not employed elsewhere.

Three-fourths of the respondents indicated that a majority of their part-time faculty were employed elsewhere, either full-time or part-time. These data paint a very obvious picture of persons who devote the majority of their time to pursuits other than teaching in the junior college. This was particularly the case for the independent, for-profit colleges, where 100 percent reported that a majority of their part-time faculty are employed elsewhere, primarily full-time. Independent nonprofit and church-related colleges responded at the rate of 80 percent and 67 percent, respectively. Whether these facts indicate a positive or negative effect on the quality of teaching is the subject of needed research.

Compensation

Salary. There are many reasons for employing part-time faculty in the private junior college, some of which will be explored later in this chapter. One frequently encountered is that it is a cost-saving measure. Part-time faculty often complain that they are embarrassingly underpaid, and full-time faculty complain that the institutions are refusing to employ other full-time faculty because it is cheaper to use part-time faculty, most of whom assume no institutional service beyond classroom teaching. To determine to what extent prevailing salaries paid to part-time faculty bear on these issues, eighty-four private junior colleges in the 1981 and 1986 studies were asked to share information about the average salaries they paid to part-time faculty. Data from the 1986 study showed that 10 percent paid their part-time faculty an average of less than $500 per section; 15 percent paid $500 to $750; 35 percent paid $750 to $1,000; and 40 percent paid more than $1,000. Sixty-seven percent of the for-profit colleges paid salaries less than $1,000, compared to 62 percent of the church-related and 54 percent of the nonprofit colleges.

Given the fact that only 40 percent of the reporting institutions paid more than $1,000 per section, the cost of five sections per semester taught by part-time faculty is much less than that of those same five sections taught by a full-time faculty member. As a comparison of the data from the 1981 study and the 1986 study also revealed, a larger percentage of colleges paid higher amounts per course in 1986 than in 1981. However, in both studies, 10 percent of the colleges reported paying less than $500 per course. These data seem to support the concerns of both part-time and full-time faculty.

Fringe Benefits. The fringe benefits of a position may compensate for lack of an adequate salary in many cases; however, for part-time faculty in the private junior college, this is not the case. In the 1986 study of eighty-four private junior colleges, only 6 percent reported that part-time faculty received the same fringe benefits as did full-time faculty.

The remaining seventy-nine institutions reported that part-time faculty did not receive such things as paid insurance, retirement benefits, sick leave, or faculty development support. No significant differences existed in the findings of the 1981 and 1986 studies.

Offices. Compensation for services rendered may take many forms other than money. Clerical assistance, telephone service, parking, and other benefits are also forms of compensation. Having an office is one very important indicator of the degree of esteem granted to part-time faculty.

In the 1986 study, only one-third of the colleges provided offices for all part-time faculty. Another 39 percent provided offices for some—but not all—of them. Twenty-eight percent made no provision for offices for any part-time faculty.

The 1981 study showed that nearly half of all responding institutions provided offices for all part-time faculty. It is possible that the decline during the five years separating these two studies is due to the increased use of part-time faculty and the inability to provide office space for all of them.

The type of private junior college that did the least to provide office space was the independent, for-profit college. Only 17 percent provided offices for any part-time faculty, while 78 percent of the church-related colleges and 76 percent of the nonprofit colleges provided office space for some or all of the part-time faculty.

Conclusion

Reasons for Employment. There are many reasons why part-time faculty are employed in private junior colleges. Literature on the use of part-time faculty discusses some of the more frequently mentioned reasons, and administrators in research studies have added additional reasons. The 1986 study asked private junior college administrators to rank those reasons as to how much they contributed to the employment of part-time faculty.

What was the primary reason? Forty-six percent of the respondents listed the ability to accommodate enrollments that did not justify full-time faculty as their main reason for using part-time faculty. Two sets of conditions existed to cause this:

1. There were extra sections of certain courses, but not enough to warrant employing another full-time faculty member.
2. There were not enough courses in a single discipline to justify employing a full-time faculty member in that discipline.

Less frequently listed reasons, in ranked order, are as follows:

1. To acquire competent persons in the fields where full-time faculty were not available (23 percent)
2. To meet off-campus or evening class needs (17 percent)
3. To achieve curricular flexibility (7 percent)
4. To effect financial savings (5 percent)
5. To secure faculty who are kept current by their daily work (2 percent).

A comparison of these findings with the 1981 study reveals some interesting differences. In 1981, the main reason given for the employment of part-time faculty was to secure competent persons in fields where full-time faculty were not available. In 1986, that reason ranked second, indicating that more full-time faculty members must have become available in many fields. In 1981, the second-ranked reason was to achieve curricular flexibility; by 1986, that reason had slipped to fourth place, again indicating the availability of full-time faculty in a wider variety of fields.

In 1981, the third most frequently ranked reason was to effect financial savings to the institution, which ranked fifth in the 1986 study. Have financial conditions improved so dramatically as to cause that change, or has the increased use of part-time faculty caused a reluctance to rank that reason as a major one?

Two reasons that tied for sixth place in the 1981 study but were not ranked by any respondent in 1986 are (1) to protect full-time faculty in case of enrollment decline and (2) to broaden the community base by involving more persons in the college program.

Advantages and Disadvantages. Most of the reasons listed by administrators for employing part-time faculty are viewed as advantages to the institution. Succinctly stated, the employment of part-time faculty results in both academic and economic flexibility for an institution (American Association of University Professors, 1981). Academic flexibility results when part-time faculty are used to offer off-campus classes, to provide classes at unusual hours, to provide career-centered courses necessitating experienced practitioners as teachers, or to initiate a new program when enrollment is not sufficient to justify the employment of full-time faculty. Economic flexibility results because savings occur in initial salary, fringe benefits, salary increases, physical plant provisions, staff development costs, and long-term financial commitment.

Disadvantages of part-time faculty employment are most often seen from the points of view of the part-timers themselves and of their full-time colleagues. Part-timers see their compensation, in all areas, as meager; full-timers see part-timers as failing to perform the complete job of a faculty member by only meeting classes. From the perspective of the institution, disadvantages may result in only a few areas. One is the necessity of finding, interviewing, employing, supervising, and monitoring a larger number of persons than would be necessary if only full-time faculty were used. A second area of concern is whether part-time faculty lower the quality of education.

Much has been written about the quality-of-instruction issue, but few definitive data have been collected. If factors such as formal education, teaching experience, faculty meeting attendance, committee participation, student advisement, staff development participation, and the like are contributors to effective instruction, then part-time faculty will not be as effective as full-time because they are less qualified in most of these areas.

However, when efforts are made to determine whether students achieve higher or lower when they are taught by part-time or full-time faculty, the findings are surprising. Very few efforts have been made to conduct such research, but one such study compared the achievement of students in nineteen sections of English taught by part-time faculty with that of students in nineteen sections taught by full-time faculty. The students' grades and scores on an exit exam in their next English class were used to compare the two groups. The study revealed no differences between the two groups (Davis and others, 1986).

A study reported in 1984 surveyed six significant groups of educators across the nation who were knowledgeable about the two-year college to determine if the image of the junior college had changed during the 1970s (Smith and Beck, 1984). One item questioned whether the larger proportion of part-time faculty being used had a positive or negative impact on the image of the two-year college.

The six categories of respondents were community college presidents, school superintendents in communities with two-year colleges, state administrators of two-year colleges, chief state school officers, professors of community college education, and board members and staff of the American Association of Community and Junior Colleges. In no category did a majority feel that the increased use of part-time faculty had a positive impact on the image of the two-year college. The community college presidents felt most positively about the increased use of part-time faculty, and the professors of community college education felt most negatively. Although these data only record perceptions, they do represent feelings of knowledgeable persons and may reflect generally held opinions about the desirability of using more part-time faculty.

A Final Word. Despite the ready list of disadvantages as well as advantages in employing part-time faculty in private junior colleges, the data currently available seem to point toward continuing the practice. It appears obvious, then, that the task of all those involved in the private junior colleges—administrators, faculty, staff, and students—is to work toward enhancing the benefits and reducing the detriments of the practice. Private junior colleges have a long history of success in overcoming obstacles of all kinds; they should be able to make the use of part-time faculty a more beneficial practice.

References

American Association of Community and Junior Colleges. *Community, Technical, and Junior College Directory.* Washington, D.C.: American Association of Community and Junior Colleges, 1976–1986.

American Association of Junior Colleges. *1969 Junior College Directory.* Washington, D.C.: American Association of Junior Colleges, 1969.

American Association of University Professors. "The Status of Part-Time Faculty." *Academe: Bulletin of the AAUP,* 1981, *67,* 31.

Davis, D., and others. "Comparing the Achievement of Students Taught by Part-Time Versus Full-Time Faculty." *Community/Junior College Quarterly of Research and Practice*, 1986, *10*, 65-72.

Smith, M. L. *Part-Time Faculty in Private Junior Colleges*. Los Angeles: ERIC Clearinghouse for Junior Colleges, University of California, November 1981. (ED 211 141)

Smith, M. L. *Part-Time Faculty in Private Junior Colleges: 1985-1986*. Los Angeles: ERIC Clearinghouse for Junior Colleges, University of California, November 1986. (ED 274 403)

Smith, M. L., and Beck, J. J. "Image of the Community College During the 1970s: A Study of Perceptions." *Community/Junior College Quarterly of Research and Practice*, 1984, *8*, 241-243.

Snyder, T. D. *Digest of Educational Statistics, 1987*. Washington, D.C.: U.S. Government Printing Office, 1987.

Milton L. Smith is professor of educational administration at Southwest Texas State University, San Marcos, Texas.

After strengths and weaknesses are tallied and economic and demographic trends factored in, is there a future for the eighty-nine remaining private liberal arts junior colleges in the United States?

Doubts About the Future of the Private Liberal Arts Junior College

Robert H. Woodroof

The past four decades have seen a significant decline in both the number of private junior colleges and the number of students attending them. Yet the private junior college continues to fight against weaknesses and the general forces of economics and demographics that threaten its future. Amid these weaknesses are solid strengths that have supported the private junior college in the face of formidable obstacles. Both the major strengths and the weaknesses will be reviewed in light of the trend of decline to present an accurate picture of the dilemma facing the relatively few remaining private liberal arts junior colleges.

Advocates of the private junior college include students who have been fortunate enough to experience this very personal form of higher education; parents of these students; current faculty, administration, staff, and board members who have devoted their professional lives to the educational purposes of their institutions; and others who have enjoyed triple benefits as student, faculty member, and administrator. To these advocates, the idea of the demise of the private junior college is particularly distasteful.

Yet even with the characteristic diversity of higher education that has made this country's system the envy of the nations, there may come a time in the near future when there are simply too few resources, too few students, and too few faculty members willing to work at poverty income levels to support the private junior college. How ironic it is that the one type of institution most threatened with survival is the one that ushered in the egalitarian movement offering higher education to the masses in the late nineteenth and early twentieth centuries.

Revealing Statistics

Today there are fewer than one hundred private junior colleges in the United States. In fact, there is evidence of only eighty-nine institutions operating as private liberal arts junior colleges, with a total enrollment of 46,720 (Peterson's Annual Guide, 1988). (Ricks College in Idaho, with an estimated enrollment of 6,880 students, is an outlier in this study, having an enrollment more than three times larger than the nearest competitor. Ricks College is excluded from these figures to eliminate the skewing that would present a less than accurate picture of the current state of affairs for the private junior college.)

From 1950 to the present, a time during which the total number of colleges and universities in America doubled and the number of students quadrupled, private junior colleges declined in number and in students by 75 and 55 percent, respectively. Of the eighty-nine surviving institutions, more than two-thirds have enrollments of fewer than six hundred students, 55 percent have enrollments of fewer than five hundred students, and more than four of ten have enrollments of fewer than four hundred students. Only 10 percent (nine institutions) have enrollments of a thousand or more.

The average enrollment is 525 students; the median is 459. Many of these colleges have experienced serious declines in enrollment; some have stayed roughly the same in size for the past quarter-century, fluctuating above and below their current levels by 5 to 10 percent; a few have experienced growth.

Of these eighty-nine institutions, 54 percent are coed with average enrollments of 491, 33 percent are single-sex institutions with average enrollments of 495, and 13 percent have recently become coed but are still primarily single-sex institutions with average enrollments of 753 students.

The average age of these institutions is eighty years, although more than one-third were founded as academies or are "decapitated" four-year colleges founded before the era of the junior college. Thirty-four institutions (38 percent) that were established between 1890 and 1945, during the growth period for the private junior college, are still operating; twenty-four (27 percent) were founded during the period of decline from 1946 to 1989. Those institutions founded before 1890 have average enrollments of 566; the figure is 538 for those founded during the period of growth and 434 for those founded since 1946. As might be expected, the younger institutions tend to have fewer students.

It is important to note that the youngest private junior college still in existence began operations in 1975. Before 1975, the longest break in founding dates for those institutions established since 1889 was six years, which occurred between 1909 and 1915. The average break is only two years. However, it has been fourteen years since the last private junior college in existence was founded, a span of infertility that is unprecedented in junior college history.

Finances: A Catch-22

Balancing the budget of a private junior college is a major feat in itself and has monopolized the efforts of administrators since the beginning of the junior college movement. Establishing a private college of any kind is always a leap of faith, but for the private junior college, launching out in faith is an annual event. After the exciting pomp and circumstance of inaugurating a new institution is over, the realities of day-to-day operation and budget balancing become critical. "Revenue" and "expenses" are the key words that determine how and if a private junior college will grow and have often served as the simple epitaph of a little college that struggled mightily, in vain, to survive.

Revenue Issues

Student Costs. A few missionary-minded institutions in the early years had sufficient church support to forgo charging tuition to their students. Most private junior colleges, however, have relied heavily on tuition and fees as the chief source of operating capital. With an average of 90 percent of their students living in campus housing, income from room and board also helps defray the costs of operation.

While there is virtually no readily available documentation to review trends in student costs through the years, random statements in several publications paint a reliable picture of the growth of student costs. (See Table 1.)

Tuition costs experienced stable growth through the 1950s, averaging 5 to 7 percent compounded annually. Since that time, tuition has jumped 10 percent per year, compounded annually. Additionally, today's tuition has four times the effect on average family income that it had in 1900.

Table 1. Student Costs at Private Junior Colleges, 1900–1986

	Tuition			Total Cost
Year	Low	High	Average	Estimate (Avg.)
1900	$ 0	$ 60	$ 20	$ 75
1930	0	700	150	400
1957	0	1,200	500	1,062
1986	0	8,300	4,800	6,900

Sources: Extracted from Eells, 1931; Hillway, 1958; Brubacher and Rudy, 1976; Straughn and Straughn, 1983.

Endowment. Private junior colleges in the early part of the century fared much better than they do today in terms of endowment income. By 1930, one-third of all private junior colleges reported endowments between $1,000 and $1.25 million (Eells, 1931). The economic ups and downs through the years—matched by costs that continue to escalate faster than tuition can possibly respond—have forced private junior colleges to either use the capital from what little endowment they had or to concentrate on obtaining "now" money to the exclusion of raising "insurance" money for endowment. The realities of rapidly rising utilities, insurance, and building and maintenance costs have relegated endowments to a future role for most private junior colleges.

Expense Issues

Due to typically small enrollments at private junior colleges, expense allocations take on a different shape than those of larger senior colleges and universities or even public junior colleges. For example, it takes just as much administrative staff support to operate a school of two hundred students as it does for one twice that size or larger. Even though the average enrollment is 525 at today's private junior colleges, nearly six of ten institutions have enrollments of fewer than five hundred students.

These schools operate more inefficiently, with total costs per enrolled student greatly exceeding competitive sectors. Most of these fiscally inefficient schools have had little or no growth in the size of their enrollments for many years, and many have had serious declines. But the economic reality is this: Even level enrollments do not automatically mean level relative costs. Costs per student tend to rise more disproportionately when the enrollment is at an inefficient level (five hundred students or fewer as an estimate).

Table 2 presents a graphic example of this trend, showing the various revenue and expense categories over a seven-year period of a private junior college operating at an inefficient level. The enrollment of this sample college fluctuated around the 250-student mark during this period.

While enrollment remained steady from 1979 to 1983, averaging 252 each year, the budget jumped 106 percent, far greater than the rate of inflation for that period. The percent of the budget for academic support, student services, and plant maintenance decreased, while the percent for administration and general expenses increased 70 percent. On the revenue side, the percent for tuition and fees dropped because it was not feasible to overtax the student with the budgetary woes caused by weak enrollments. Therefore, gift income had to increase to nearly half of the total budget.

The school was able to keep pace through 1982 by increasing gift income, but in one year the year-end balance went from a positive $4,600

Table 2. Revenue/Expenses of a Private Junior College Operating at an Inefficient Enrollment Level (1977-1983)

Category	1977	1978	1979	1980	1981	1982	1983
Revenue							
Tuition/Fees	32%	31%	32%	33%	29%	25%	26%
Gift Income	37%	39%	35%	31%	40%	48%	45%
Auxiliary Sources	29%	28%	30%	32%	28%	25%	25%
Other Sources	2%	2%	3%	4%	3%	2%	4%
Expenses							
Administrative/General	32%	32%	26%	26%	37%	42%	44%
Academic Support	17%	17%	20%	18%	17%	18%	17%
Auxiliary Expenses	21%	21%	26%	26%	24%	17%	16%
Student Services	14%	14%	12%	11%	11%	11%	10%
Plant Maintenance	7%	9%	8%	9%	8%	7%	7%
Other Expenses	9%	7%	8%	10%	3%	6%	6%
Budget (in millions)	$0.63	$0.81	$1.08	$1.38	$1.68	$2.05	$2.23
Revenue Over or Under Expenses (in thousands)	$7.54	$7.80	$9.90	$8.00	$1.31	$4.60	($42.40)
Enrollment	153	182	233	273	249	262	244
Cost per Student (budgetary)	$4,117	$4,451	$4,635	$5,055	$6,747	$7,824	$9,139

to a negative $42,400. It is uncertain how long a school can survive with this burden. The tenacity and resilience of those men and women who work at schools like the one reviewed is remarkable. But one thing is certain: This story could be told many times over by just changing the name of the college.

There is an interesting caveat to this story. Many private junior colleges have trouble raising gift income to build facilities. When there is an urgent need for a new facility—or for the renovation of one that is deteriorating—the only alternative is to seek funding from other sources, such as banks or bond issues. If gift income is not forthcoming to pay these obligations, the costs of making mortgage payments, or of covering bond commitments at maturity, must come from somewhere else. With no endowment or gift income to cover construction or renovation costs, these obligations must be covered out of operating expenses. When this happens, the cost of educating each student skyrockets until the burden is unbearable.

Competition from the Community College

Private junior colleges tend to survive in areas where the community college is not particularly strong. No formal documentation proves this statement, but in California and Texas, two of the stronger community college states, there are a total of six private junior colleges (three in each state, with a total enrollment of only 2,800 students)—not a particularly strong showing (Straughn and Straughn, 1983).

Today, 72 percent of the private junior colleges and 85 percent of the students are located east of the Mississippi River. In 1930, before the community college made its presence known with force, there were nearly as many private junior colleges west of the Mississippi River as there were east. California and Texas alone had forty-two private junior colleges, attended by one of six enrolled students. The trend has reversed itself in the last five decades (Eells, 1931).

Table 3 shows the trend in the decline of the private junior college west of the Mississippi River. Even though this trend has been downward throughout the United States since 1945, the remaining strength still centers in the East.

The Strengths—Do They Outweigh the Perplexing Problems?

The two major strengths of the private junior college are (1) the high level of development they offer to the student due to true one-on-one contact with faculty, and (2) the loyalty of faculty committed to teaching.

Student Development. The acid test for determining the success of a private junior college in educating its students is how well those students do when they graduate and transfer to advanced institutions. Results of research in 1930 and 1980 suggest that "state universities have little or no grounds for the fear that the junior college . . . brings into their upper years a flood of mentally incompetent students" (Eells, 1931, p. 255).

Table 3. Trends East and West of the Mississippi River in Numbers of Private Junior Colleges and Students

	Colleges		Students		Average Enrollment	
Year	East	West	East	West	East	West
1930	146	133	16,324	14,078	112	106
1955	186	64	59,507	15,871	320	248
1988	64	25	39,940	6,780	624	271

Source: Data extracted from Eells, 1931; Straughn and Straughn, 1983; *Junior College Journal,* 1930, 1950.

In 1930, Eells concluded from a major five-year study that not only did junior college transfers from both public and private institutions perform as well as native four-year college students of the same rank, they tended to score considerably better. A second part of the study showed that junior college transfers also scored better in their last two years than in their first two years of study. The control group of four-year students performed more consistently throughout their college careers at a rate slightly beneath that of the junior college students.

Eells's study was comprehensive and national in scope, separating out the various types of junior colleges for individual comparison. The private liberal arts junior college fared as well as all others and was superior when the results of women were analyzed.

Although no such inclusive studies exist for the 1980s, independent studies by Ohio Valley College, Michigan Christian College, Northeastern Christian Junior College, and York College (Nebraska), all private junior colleges, have shown similar results. Not only do their graduates have higher grade point averages in their senior college studies than in their junior college courses, they perform equally with their native four-year college peers.

A higher percentage of private junior college graduates are also involved in extracurricular activities and win positions of leadership than their peers at senior colleges and universities. Perhaps this shows that, for many years, private junior colleges have been meeting their responsibility in preparing students for further study, and that this is one of the strengths that help these struggling schools continue to operate.

Faculty Loyalty and Love of Teaching. It is unlikely that any faculty member is in higher education to earn a large salary. Private junior college faculty members, however, either have had a remarkable missionary spirit in order to survive on the paltry salaries awarded them or have felt that they could not compete for jobs at better-paying institutions.

The missionary spirit has always played a large role in helping struggling institutions retain their best faculty and is perhaps the only thing that has helped maintain the credibility of those institutions that have survived. Private junior college faculty members are people who have learned to live on less in order to enjoy the intangible benefits of teaching in a small, comfortable environment, working with other faculty and students of similar religious backgrounds or moral beliefs, and helping the individual student succeed.

It is difficult to understand what motivates these men and women to work long hours teaching unusually heavy loads for a salary that is 32 percent less, on the average, than what their public counterparts receive. Perhaps it is partly that many are young faculty members in their first full-time teaching positions. Others are older and may feel little incentive or confidence to find a better position in terms of remuneration. And it is clear that many are simply committed to their role, regarding tough financial times as an annoying but tolerable reality.

The rapid decline of the private junior college puts the surviving institutions in great jeopardy. This is unfortunate. Thousands of junior college students are enjoying successes they may not have had otherwise because of the dedication of faculty not as interested in national acclaim or salary level as they are in the futures of their students.

Private junior college faculty may lack the perceived sophistication of senior college or university faculty, but their commitment to the liberal arts and to the role of the teacher is remarkably strong. Perhaps this strength will stay the final demise of the private junior college.

Conclusion

Is there a future for the private liberal arts junior college in American higher education? The case is most persuasive when documentation proves that these institutions are meeting the educational objectives to which they have dedicated their efforts.

They appear to have met some of these objectives, such as the claim to motivate freshmen and sophomore students more quickly and effectively than other sectors of higher education, proved by the successes of their graduates in advanced studies and leadership roles at senior colleges. And private junior colleges enjoy the benefit of perhaps the most loyal faculty in the country, who are willing to work for dismal wages in order to do what they do best: teach.

But these strengths alone are evidently not enough to curtail the rapid demise of the private junior college, brought about by two key influences: financial pressures creating a state of exigency for many schools, and competition for students from the community college. The following facts taken from the text of this chapter are hard to ignore or to dismiss as concerns that will pass in time:

1. From 1950 to 1988, a time when the number of colleges in America doubled and the number of college students quadrupled, private junior colleges declined 75 percent in number and 55 percent in students.

2. More than half of the remaining eighty-nine junior colleges have enrollments of fewer than five hundred students, considered to be an inefficient size. In fact, more than four of every ten private junior colleges have enrollments of fewer than four hundred students.

3. The low enrollment trend seems not to respect institutional type; both coed and single-sex colleges suffer. Older institutions, such as those founded before the era of the junior college—as academies or four-year colleges—tend to have higher enrollments, on the average.

4. It has been fourteen years since a surviving private junior college was last established. This is the longest period of inactivity for the found-

ing of any type of institution in the history of American higher education, save the first two hundred years of the country's development. However, it must be noted that fewer colleges of all types are being founded today, perhaps reflecting a level of saturation, given the country's current needs and economic status.

5. Endowments are minuscule or nonexistent at most private junior colleges, where "now" money gets precedence over future "insurance" money.

6. Costs per student rise disproportionately to the level of tuition increase when enrollments decrease or are stagnant, which increases the need for gift income or forces the reduction of other services for the institution to remain solvent. This is an annual fact of life for most private junior colleges.

7. Community colleges tend to force private junior colleges out of the junior college market. There are few places where community colleges and private junior colleges operate in the same community and both are viable institutions of higher education, with stable enrollments and strong financial bases. This trend is most vivid in the West, where the community college is strong but where there are virtually no private junior colleges. This situation has reversed itself since 1930.

At the rate that private junior colleges are currently closing, merging with senior colleges, or becoming senior colleges themselves, the private junior college as it is today may not survive to witness the new century. It is clear that there will be few, if any, new private junior colleges formed during the remainder of this century, and quite a few of the remaining eighty-nine institutions are contemplating four-year status as soon as that is feasible, if they can survive long enough to enact the change.

Who will survive? If the trend holds true, perhaps a few of the thirty or so colleges with current enrollments of six hundred or more students will still operate by the year 2000 A.D. Can the trend be reversed? The admonition of the American Association of Junior Colleges, made in 1963 after a study of the private junior college, suggested the need to address serious concerns, including fulfilling their educational intention:

> Private junior colleges are faced with a large set of problems of varying proportions. The greatest of these problems is the foundation of clear, fully defensible educational purposes and the ability to communicate them to a wide variety of publics. With this problem, and an integral part of it, is the obtaining of sufficient resources—both human and financial—to bring these purposes to life in ways not universally available to these colleges.
>
> The destiny of America's private junior college[s] hinges on the extent to which they are able . . . to fulfill their educational intention.

The private junior college of today is fulfilling its educational intention, in theory, by providing the first two years of quality education and preparation for more advanced study. It is accomplishing these goals very well, with an impressive track record of graduates who move on to senior colleges to earn higher grades and serve in leadership roles. However, since the publishing of the above declaration twenty-six years ago, the number of private junior colleges has declined from 278 to 89, a decrease of 68 percent. The practical side of educational intention is to do these things well *and in a fiscally responsible manner.* Perhaps the true destiny of private junior colleges is determined by "the extent to which they are able to fulfill their educational intention [in a fiscally responsible manner]." All current trends suggest a bleak future for the typical private junior college. Perhaps the American system of higher education has outgrown the need for private education at the two-year level, having made other arrangements for the millions of younger and older adults who seek the resources of the two-year college. After nearly forty-five years of decline, we have entered the decade of decision for the private junior college.

References

American Association of Junior Colleges. *The Privately Supported Junior College: A Place and Purpose in Higher Education.* Washington, D.C.: American Association of Junior Colleges, 1963.

Brubacher, J. S., and Rudy, W. *Higher Education in Transition.* New York: Harper & Row, 1976.

Eells, W. C. *The Junior College.* Boston: Houghton Mifflin, 1931.

Hillway, T. *The American Two-Year College.* New York: Harper & Row, 1958.

Peterson's Annual Guide to Undergraduate Study. Princeton, N.J.: Peterson's Guides, 1988.

Straughn, C. T., and Straughn, B. L. (eds.). *Lovejoy's College Guide.* (16th ed.) New York: Monarch Press, 1983.

Robert H. Woodroof is assistant professor of communication at Pepperdine University, Malibu, California.

INDEX

Academic college, 4
Adler, L., 22, 32
Affective domain, 37-38
American Association of Community and Junior Colleges, 81, 84, 91, 92
American Association of Junior Colleges, 101, 102
American Association of University Professors, 90, 92
American College Test (ACT): for faculty, 35-36; at Ohio Valley College, 36, 39-40
Anderson, R. D., 29, 32
Armstrong, J. L., 57, 64
Assessment, 41-42; approach to, 38-41; areas for, 34-36; of cognitive versus affective domains, 37-38; past methods of, 33-34; and pretests, 36-37
Association of American Colleges, 11, 17
Astin, A. W., 56, 64
Austin, N., 63, 65

Baker, G. A. III, 53, 65
Bangert-Drowns, R. L., 74, 78
Barton, D. W., Jr., 21, 22, 28, 32
Beck, J. J., 91, 92
Bell, E., 72, 77
Berger, C., 70, 77
Berger, C. F., 72, 79
Bergquist, W. H., 57, 64
Bernard, F. A., 71, 79
Blom, K. G., 72, 77
Bok, D., 62, 64
Bowen, H. R., 10-11, 17, 56, 59, 64
Bowker, L. S., 71, 77
Bowker, R. C., 71, 77
Boyer, E. L., 62, 64
Brademas, J., 12, 17
Brawer, F. B., 55, 64
Brillhart, L. V., 72, 77
Brown, M., 73, 77
Brubacher, J. S., 3, 4, 7, 95, 102
Bunderson, C. V., 73, 78

Campbell, C. C., 27, 32
Cater, D., 16, 17

Chickering, A. W., 55, 64
Christensen, D. L., 76, 78
Church-related junior colleges, 53-54; expanding enrollment of, 54-64
Coburn, P., 70, 77
Cognitive domain, 37-38
Cohen, A. M., 55, 64
Cohen, M., 75, 78
Cokewood, D., 74, 77
College(s): academic, 4; church-related junior, 53-64; community, 5, 97-98, 91; junior, 4, 43, 67-77; private, 10-12, 15-16; public, 12; public junior, 5-6; senior, 4; two-year, 10, 81; university, 4. *See also* Private junior college(s)
College-Level Examination Program, 38, 42
Communication: at church-related junior colleges, 61-62; and marketing, 23, 25, 27-28
Community college, 5; as competition, 97-98, 101. *See also* Junior college; Two-year college
Community, Technical, and Junior College Directory, 82, 83, 85
COMOL, 73-74
Computer literacy, 75
Computer-assisted instruction (CAI), 68-69, 73-74, 75, 76, 77
Computer-managed instruction (CMI), 69
Computers, 76-77; academic potential of, 74-76; effectiveness of, 73-74; trends in use of, 67-73
Core curriculum, 34
Cost, of education, 11-13

Dartmouth College decision, 15
Davis, D., 91, 92
Decapitation, 4
Dickmeyer, N., 11, 17
Diener, T., 3, 7
Differentiation, 30-31
Division of Higher Education, 58, 64
Dunham, J. L., 73, 78

93

Education: cost of, 11-13; values approach to, 10-11
Eells, W. C., 6, 7, 95, 96, 98-99, 102
Eindhoven, University of, 69
Ellinger, R. S., 73, 77
Ellis, J. D., 68, 70, 77
Emck, J. H., 69, 77
Endowment, 95-96
Engledow, J. L., 29, 32
Enrollment: expanding, at church-related colleges, 43-54; inefficient, and finances, 97; trends in, 13-14
Evaluation: and marketing, 23, 25, 28-30

Faculty: full-time versus part-time, 83; loyalty of, 99-100; in private junior colleges, 85; testing of, 35-36
Faculty, part-time: characteristics of, 86-88; compensation of, 88-89; expectations of, 84-86; at private junior colleges, 82-84, 85, 89-91; at two-year colleges, 81
Ferguson-Hessler, M.G.M., 69, 77
Fields, G. D., Jr., 1, 53, 65
Finances: of church-related junior colleges, 60; of private junior colleges, 95-97; of public colleges, 12
Frankland, P., 73, 77

Gagné, R. M., 69, 77
Garson, G. D., 75, 77
Geltzer, H., 27, 32
General education, 34-35
Goles, G. G., 70, 71, 77
Grabe, M., 74, 78

Hajovy, H., 76, 78
Harper, W. R., 4, 43
Heard, J. T., Jr., 71, 78
Henderson, J., 71-72
Hepner, G. F., 72, 78
Hillway, T., 95, 102
Hirsch, E. D., Jr., 13, 17, 35, 42
Hodgkinson, H. L., 13, 17, 43, 64
Hodler, T. W., 72, 78
Hoffman, N. M., 16, 17
Hoffman, N. M., Jr., 1, 9, 17
Hollen, T. T., Jr., 73, 78

Howard, J. A., 10, 17
Hsiao, M. W., 72, 78
Huddleston, T., 29, 32
Hutchins, R. M., 10, 17

Ihlanfeldt, W., 22, 27, 32
Innovation, 31-32
Interactive video, 75-76

Johnson, D. L., 22, 32
Junior college, 4, 43; church-related, 53-64; public, 5-6; use of computers in, 67-77. *See also* Community college; Private junior college(s); Two-year college
Junior College Journal, 6, 7, 98
Junior College Directory, 83, 92

Kotler, P., 22, 26, 32-33
Kulik, C. C., 74, 78
Kulik, J. A., 74, 78

LaBaugh, T., 27, 33
Lasell Female Academy, 5
Lasell Junior College, 5
Lehman, J. D., 76, 78
Levin, J. A., 75, 78
Liberal arts, 10, 14
Litten, L. H., 22, 33

McGrath, E. J., 16, 17
McMahon, H., 73, 77
Mahoney, J. R., 54, 65
Marketing, 19-21; model of, 21-30; trends in, 30-32
Marks, G. H., 75, 78
Mayhew, L. B., 12, 17
Michigan Christian College, 99
Microcomputer-based labs (MBLs), 72
Mitchell, P. T., 1, 19, 33
Moore, J. F., 69, 78

Nakhleh, M. B., 67, 70, 78
National Association of Independent Colleges and Universities (NAICU), 21

National Commission on Excellence in Education, 67, 78
National Commission on United Methodist Higher Education, 15, 17
National Council of Independent Junior Colleges (NCIJC), 21, 30, 31
National Institute of Independent Colleges and Universities, 11-12, 13, 16, 17
National Science Foundation, 76
National Videodisc Symposium, 76
Northeast Missouri State University, 39, 42
Northeastern Christian Junior College, 99

O'Brien, T. C., 75, 78
Ohio Valley College, 38, 39; ACT at, 35, 36, 39-40
Okey, J. A., 74, 78
Okey, J. R., 70, 78

Parker, C. A., 59, 65
Parnell, D., 49, 55
Peters, T., 63, 65
Peterson's Annual Guide, 94, 102
Planning, at church-related junior colleges, 56-57, 61-62
Pluralism, 15-16
Presidents, on future, 14-15
Pretests, risks of, 36-37
Private colleges: finances of, 11-12; and pluralism, 15-16; values education at, 10-11
Private junior college(s), 3; church-related, 53-64; competition for, 97-98; and computers, 67-77; and cost of education, 11-13; enrollment in, 13-14; finances of, 95-97; future of, 1-2, 9, 16-17, 93, 100-102; history of, 4-7; marketing of, 19-32; part-time faculty at, 81-91; and pluralism, 15-16; presidents' views on, 14-15; statistics on, 94-95; strengths of, 98-100. *See also* Junior college
Program, and marketing, 23, 24-25, 26-27
Public colleges, finances of, 12
Public junior college, history of, 5-6

Queen, J. A., 70, 78

Randall, J. E., 68, 70, 78
Reinecker, L., 70, 78
Reis, A., 27, 32
Religion. *See* Church-related junior colleges
Research, for marketing, 22, 23, 24, 26
Retained knowledge, 35-36
Rojas, A., 69, 77
Ross, K. A., 55, 60, 61, 65
Roueche, J. E., 53, 65
Rudy, W., 3, 4, 7, 95, 102
Ryan, P., 71, 78

Saint Paul's College, 6
Salomon, G., 74, 78
Sargent, F. P., 5, 7
Senior college, 4
Shaw, E. L., 70, 78
Simulations, computer, 69-70
Smith, M. L., 2, 81, 82, 91, 92
Snyder, T. D., 81, 92
Spartanburg Methodist College, 54-64
Straughn, B. L., 6, 7, 95, 98, 102
Straughn, C. T., 6, 7, 95, 98, 102
Student body: expanding, at church-related colleges, 53-64
Suder, R., 72, 79
Sullivan, D. F., 22, 33
Switzer, T. J., 70, 73, 79
Sybouts, W., 76, 79

Taylor model, of computer use, 68
Taylor, R. P., 68, 70, 79
Testing. *See* Assessment
Thomas, W. E., 68, 73, 79
Thompson, S. R., 71, 79
Tinker, R. F., 72, 79
Treadwell, D. R., Jr., 28, 32
Tritz, G. J., 70, 71, 79
Tuition, at private junior colleges, 95
Two-year college: future dominance of, 10; part-time faculty at, 81. *See also* Community college; Junior college

University college, 4

Value(s): of church-related colleges, 54-56; and private colleges, 10-11

Wager, W., 69, 77
Warlick, C. H., 75, 79
Warren Wilson College, 50
Waugh, M. L., 70, 74, 78, 79
Webster, D., 15
Wells, G. L., 2, 67, 72, 79
West, D. C., 15, 17

White, C. S., 70, 73, 79
Wholeben, B. E., 75, 77, 79
Williams, J. H., 1, 33, 42
Wilson, T. H., 5, 7
Wolfe, C., 75
Woodroof, R. H., 2, 3, 7, 93, 102
Word processors, 71

York College, 99

Zamora, R. M., 70, 79
Zucker, A. A., 76, 79

Ordering Information

NEW DIRECTIONS FOR COMMUNITY COLLEGES is a series of paperback books that offers guidelines and programs for aiding students in their total development—emotional, social, physical, as well as intellectual. Books in the series are published quarterly in Fall, Winter, Spring, and Summer and are available for purchase by subscription as well as by single copy.

SUBSCRIPTIONS for 1990 cost $48.00 for individuals (a savings of 20 percent over single-copy prices) and $64.00 for institutions, agencies, and libraries. Please do not send institutional checks for personal subscriptions. Standing orders are accepted.

SINGLE COPIES cost $14.95 when payment accompanies order. (California, New Jersey, New York, and Washington, D.C., residents please include appropriate sales tax.) Billed orders will be charged postage and handling.

DISCOUNTS FOR QUANTITY ORDERS are available. Please write to the address below for information.

ALL ORDERS must include either the name of an individual or an official purchase order number. Please submit your order as follows:
 Subscriptions: specify series and year subscription is to begin
 Single copies: include individual title code (such as CC1)

MAIL ALL ORDERS TO:
 Jossey-Bass Inc., Publishers
 350 Sansome Street
 San Francisco, California 94104

OTHER TITLES AVAILABLE IN THE
NEW DIRECTIONS FOR COMMUNITY COLLEGES SERIES
Arthur M. Cohen, Editor-in-Chief
Florence B. Brawer, Associate Editor

CC68 Alternative Funding Sources, *James L. Catanzaro, Allen D. Arnold*
CC67 Perspectives on Student Development, *William L. Deegan, Terry O'Banion*
CC66 Using Student Tracking Systems Effectively, *Trudy H. Bers*
CC65 A Search for Institutional Distinctiveness, *Barbara K. Townsend*
CC64 External Influences on the Curriculum, *David B. Wolf, Mary Lou Zoglin*
CC63 Collaborating with High Schools, *Janet E. Lieberman*
CC62 Issues in Personnel Management, *Richard I. Miller, Edward W. Holzapfel, Jr.*
CC61 Enhancing Articulation and Transfer, *Carolyn Prager*
CC60 Marketing Strategies for Changing Times, *Wellford W. Wilms, Richard W. Moore*
CC59 Issues in Student Assessment, *Dorothy Bray, Marcia J. Belcher*
CC58 Developing Occupational Programs, *Charles R. Doty*
CC57 Teaching the Developmental Education Student, *Kenneth M. Ahrendt*
CC56 Applying Institutional Research, *John Losak*
CC55 Advances in Instructional Technology, *George H. Voegel*
CC54 The Community College and Its Critics, *L. Stephen Zwerling*
CC53 Controversies and Decision Making in Difficult Economic Times, *Billie Wright Dziech*